HE

ALSO BY FLORENCE KING

Southern Ladies and Gentlemen

Wasp, Where Is Thy Sting?

HE

An Irreverent Look

at the American Male

FLORENCE KING

 STEIN AND DAY/*Publishers*/New York

For a very special Forty-Niner

Our lives are Swiss, so cool, so still,
Till some odd afternoon
The Alps neglect their curtains
And we look farther on.

—Emily Dickinson

First published in 1978
Copyright © 1978 by Florence King
All rights reserved
Designed by L. Hebard
Printed in the United States of America
Stein and Day/*Publishers*/Scarborough House,
Briarcliff Manor, N.Y. 10510
Some of the material in this book has appeared in
slightly different form in *Cosmopolitan, Playgirl,* and *MS.*

Library of Congress Cataloging in Publication Data

King, Florence.
He: An Irreverent Look at the American Male

    1. Men—United States.   I. Title.
HQ1090.K56   301.41′1′0973   78-7464
ISBN 0-8128-2513-6

CONTENTS

Let other pens dwell on guilt and misery.

—Jane Austen, *Mansfield Park*

AUTHOR'S NOTE
or I Changed All the Names

Some of the men I have known are living, some are dead, and a few have been shockingly coincidental, but in every case I have been meticulous about shielding the identities of the guilty. The only person I have libeled is myself. Everyone else has been new-baptized.

Anyone who is as contemptuous of sociological "writing" as I am will be happy to know that these pages contain no charts, no graphs, no cluster groupings, and no percentiles of North-eastern Seaboard men who have done naughty things to my sliding scale. This sort of science àgo-go is one of the major problems between the sexes today, and I react to it with the same scorn that Rollo May felt when his psychologist friend said: "The trouble with Romeo and Juliet was that they hadn't had adequate counseling." *

In anticipation of the distress that my consistent use of *Miss* will cause, I should like to explain that I am sick of *Ms.* I agree with Archie Bunker; it sounds like a bug. It also offends my writer's instincts. An abbreviation is supposed to be a short-ened form of *something*. *Ms.* is a shortened form of *nothing*. There is no one specific word behind it except *manuscript*. I

---

* *Love and Will.*

prefer to be called *Miss* because I am a spinster—still the proper legal term for never-married women in sensible England. In these pages I have referred to writers and other prominent women as *Miss* regardless of their marital status because they have all excelled in some way independently of men. Thus they have earned the privilege of going by the spinster's honorific.

In a review of my last book, *Wasp, Where Is Thy Sting?* a critic wrote: "You will find nothing in Florence King's book to offend you unless you are nativist or ethnic, rich or poor, black or white, Catholic or Protestant, northerner or southerner, liberal or conservative, male or female. All others beware."

Caveat lector, for this is the same kind of book. I am neither feminist nor Total Woman, just sick of both. I merely think that men are the funniest things since silly putty.

HE

1

VIRGIN SPRING
or My Life Before Men

When a woman writes a book critical of men, her psyche is analyzed relentlessly by people who have never met her. At cocktail parties or during the entr'acte at the madrigal concert, pseudosophisticates of the "Aha!" persuasion put her on the couch and conclude that she is bitter because of something dreadful that happened during her childhood to turn her against the male sex.

To nip such fabrications in the bud, I shall begin by telling you the truth about my childhood. It was idyllic. Neither of my parents ever tried to influence my developing sexual psychology. The fourth member of our household was in charge of my mental health. As soon as "Inner Sanctum" came on the radio, my grandmother would lead me off to bed, saying, "I don't want this child to grow up warped." When she had tucked me in, she would sing me to sleep with the ballads of her youth:

> *She is more to be pitied than censured,*
> *She is more to be helped than despised,*
> *She's only a lassie who ventured*
> *On life's stormy path ill-advised;*
> *Do not scorn her with words fierce and bitter,*

1

Do not laugh at her shame and downfall;
For a moment just stop and consider
That a man was the cause of it all!

I drifted off to sleep with visions of women who were wrecks upon life's sea, who loved and paid the cost, who lived in a mansion of aching hearts, who were cast aside like a toy, and in one case—"She May Have Seen Better Days"—a ruined woman who rolled in the gutter while a crowd of men laughed at her.

Instead of frightening me or giving me an inferiority complex, Granny's songs made men seem a bit jejune. Women, on the other hand, were tremendously important, the invariable center of great swirling dramas and snowstorms. There was a broken female heart for every light on Broadway, and every coffin taken off a baggage coach had a woman in it. There was a woman buried in the shade of the old apple tree, not a man. It was a daughter who telephoned her dead mother with "Hello, Central, Give Me Heaven," and Central was a woman, too. After that one, I never quite believed that men were better at solving mechanical problems. Granny never sang songs about men, so I concluded that they were not very important people. Their sole function, I knew, was throwing themselves across fresh graves, and even that was a poor substitute because no matter how hard men tried, they could never be fallen women.

My conviction that the world was dominated and run by size-44 goddesses was strengthened by the influence of my honorary grandmother, Emma, the janitor's wife who worked for us. Emma was a Lily of the Valley at her church, and held meetings with the other Lilies in her apartment. Once I looked in on them, and except for skin color, they all looked like Granny.

Emma's opinion of men was, shall we say, unenthusiastic, but she thought the sun rose and set with Granny. Whenever

Granny made an observation or expressed an opinion, no matter how trivial, Emma would point her finger in my face and say: "You listen to yo' Big Momma. She tellin' it."

Neither of them was at all passive in the traditional feminine manner. In fact, they were both egomaniacs, an aberration never more in evidence than when they performed for the passengers on the 11th and Monroe streetcar. Emma often got on at Irving Street, where her church was located, when Granny and I were coming home from downtown. When they saw each other, they mugged elaborate surprise and then went into their Weber & Fields routine:

"Miss Lura! Where you been?"

"I been to the beauty parlor to get my hair curled. Where you been, Emma?"

"I been to the beauty parlor to get mine straightened!"

This always brought forth gales of laughter from the other passengers. They were applauded more than once, especially when they did their imitation of the Dolly Sisters, which was better, if not quite so glamorous, as the Betty Grable–June Haver version at the neighborhood movie. When the motorman rang his bell and carried us up the street, I decided that he, like all men, was merely a stagehand in the service of life's superstars.

Except for my father, I knew very few men. From kindergarten through high school I never had a male teacher or even a male principal. In those days of fusty, lace-fichued spinsters, most of my teachers even looked like Granny, so I regarded them as still more honorary grandmothers. My concept of the world as a matriarchy was complete the day I found out the truth about my favorite radio personality. I asked Granny, "What grade is Baby Snooks in?" She laughed and replied, "Why, she's my age. I saw her on the stage years and years ago." I refused to believe this until she showed me a newspaper photo of the real Baby Snooks. That did it: life was one big grandmother, and I was as secure as a fledgling butterfly in a cocoon.

I was convinced that women were not only superior, they were immortal. Like all Southerners we went visiting a lot, and in many homes we ran into a typically Southern situation. The door was opened by an old lady in her seventies, who turned around and shouted: "Mama! We got company!" In the living room we paid our respects to the nonagenarian Mama, who then summoned her youngest daughter, a woman in her sixties known as Little Sis, and asked her to bring refreshments. Little Sis returned with a tray containing ladylike sherry for the guests and the daughters of the house, "something for the child" for me, and a fifth of 100-proof Virginia Gentleman for the nonagenarian Mama. "Heart," said Mama in explanation, fluttering a papery hand to her breast. "The doctor told me to take a little stimulant." Everyone nodded respectfully.

It is at this moment, when she is knocking back her first snort, that the antediluvian Southern woman recites the woeful tale of her lifelong battle against poor health. It starts with her premature birth. She was *always* a seven-months baby. Whether she actually was or not makes no difference because she has come to believe it. "They said I wouldn't last the winter. People told my mother, 'You'll never raise that one. If the Lord takes her it'll be for the best.' " Everyone nods respectfully, which encourages her to continue her saga about the many times she *almost* died. Still sipping straight bourbon, she confides to her audience that all the women in her family are plagued with delicate constitutions.

There were never any men in the homes we visited. They had all died somewhere between forty and fifty, felled by the rigors of chivalry, leaving fragile, helpless, desperately ill widows to "cope"—the Southern woman's favorite verb—as best they could.

I spent nearly every Sunday of my formative years in such homes, listening to these drawling Brunhildes. What sticks in my mind most clearly is the tiny conspiratorial smile that twitches about the corners of a Southern woman's mouth when she talks about female weakness. Every Southern girlchild catches on early in the game. The message is: women are indomitable.

Our last visit of the day took us to what is now Washington's fashionable Foggy Bottom. It wasn't very fashionable then, but no Sunday went by without a visit to Emma's mother, who was 106. She looked like a voodoo doll made out of charred matchsticks and had so many cataracts that her eyes shone like highly polished white pebbles.

"How are you, Miss Jensy?" I would ask, as I presented her with the weekly can of Prince Albert that we always took her.

"Ain't nebber bin sick a day in my life," she replied, lighting her pipe.

There were no men in Miss Jensy's home, either. Once I asked her where Emma's father was and she shrugged and said, "Oh, he daid." Despite the dearth of males, she was prepared—armed is a better word—for their intrusion into her living room. Every chair was covered with spanking-white crocheted squares.

"What are those white things?" I asked her once.

"Dey called antimacassars."

"What are they for?"

She leaned forward suddenly and gave me a ferocious pebbly-white stare.

" 'Cause mens leaves spots!"

There was no doubt about it. I belonged to the superior sex.

Because we were high-church Episcopalian—known in Maryland, home of the crab, as "softshell Catholic"—I escaped Christian sexual puritanism completely. After all, the Episcopal church got its start because Anne Boleyn was a good lay. I grew up believing that devoutness was for colored people and that white people merely went to the Episcopal church once in a while. In our case, once in a while meant Christmas, Palm Sunday, Easter, and whenever Granny bought a new hat.

I sensed very early in life, with that primitive insight of children, that church was just another outlet for Granny's boundless ego. The urge to make a grand entrance was strong in her. She would wait until the very last minute, and then sail up the aisle, fall to her knees in a full genuflection, make the sign of the cross over her gigantic bosom, then settle down in the pew and go to sleep. On ordinary Sundays she stayed put, but the Easter service, which is virtually a High Mass, was much too long for her tastes so she would take my hand, sail back down the aisle, and take me to the corner drugstore for a milk shake. She always timed our split so that we would be out before they passed the plate, and when we returned she would tell people, "The child had to go to the bathroom."

I attended Sunday School a few times, where I learned to sing "Jesus Loves Me." I saw no reason why He shouldn't because I had also escaped Christian misogyny. The story of the Garden of Eden and Eve's sin eluded me, thanks to Granny's interpretation of it: "He let her talk him into it. Men are so weak. The least he could have done was to take all the blame on himself instead of tattling to God on his own wife." Most of the time, though, Granny promulgated the Book of Genesis in limerick form: "Adam and Eve and Pinch-Me-Tight went down the river to have a fight. Adam and Eve fell in the water. Who was left?"

The only Christian doctrine that sank in was Heaven. Granny talked a lot about Heaven because it figured so often in her Gay Nineties songs. Someone was always dying and going there in the third verse, so she described it in detail: it was full of pink clouds, golden stairs, sweet-voiced angels, and Saint Peter, who was in charge of the gate. That made sense—after all, men are supposed to open doors. All in all, Granny's Heaven struck me as an ultrafeminine place designed for the comfort and entertainment of women, rather like Woodward & Lothrop's tearoom between two and four in the afternoon.

It was because of this view of Heaven that I committed a terrible faux pas. It happened at the first funeral I ever attended. One of Granny's relatives died and so we all went to the undertaker's to pay our respects. Everything was very elegant and very Wasp—i.e., nobody was crying, so you could hear a pin drop. The casket contained a middle-aged male, which I considered par for the corpse, but when I heard someone whisper softly, "He was such a good man, he'll go to Heaven," I looked up at Granny in astonishment.

"Granny," I piped, in that loud, clear voice of children, "can men go to Heaven?"

Granny had what she liked to believe was a gentlewoman's conscience that took her on what she liked to call "missions of mercy." Actually they were ego trips. We spent Saturdays driving around Washington with old clothes, fruit baskets, flowers, and gallons of split pea soup which we dropped off at the jail, the Episcopal Home, St. Elizabeth's mental hospital, and Congressional Cemetery. Granny had projects who were locked in, tied up, and laid out everywhere. Her self-image being what it was, whenever she heard about a new needy case, she would tug at her girdle and drawl, "Ah'm just goin' to have to pu'form a miracle."

In her opinion, miracles began and ended with pea soup. It was her snake oil, guaranteed to cure anything from melancholia to leprosy. I knew all about what pea soup could do *for* people; one Saturday I found out what it can do *to* people; specifically to men. It was through pea soup that male vulnerability was revealed to me.

My father was terribly nice but quiet, as any son-in-law of

Granny's was bound to be. To this day I can't appreciate mother-in-law jokes because he was unfailingly polite to her, despite the fact that she was enough to fill the French Foreign Legion. I would like to think that he had a mistress but I rather doubt it. I do know that he had another comfort: his car. It was a 1940 Packard, the last model made before the war started. It was a thing of beauty with dark woolen upholstery and white-wall tires, and he loved it with all his heart.

One Saturday when the car was about a month old, we loaded it up with fruit baskets, flowers, old clothes, and a kettle of pea soup and took off on a day-long round of Christian charity. As we were crossing the Anacostia bridge on our way to our third poorhouse we hit a pothole. The pea soup tipped over and flooded the back of the car. My father pulled over to the curb and stared with stricken eyes into the back seat. The rich woolen floor covering was a mass of greenish slime, and in the middle of it all was a long white ham bone. It looked like somebody's arm; if a cop had seen it he would have booked us as acid-bath murderers.

We all squished out of the car except for my father, who put his head down on the wheel. As I stared at his hunched, defeated form I realized that he was weeping. I still see him every time I hear feminists talk about how to humanize men. It's easy: just spill pea soup all over their new cars.

It was also due to our missions of mercy that I acquired the theory that men were a mutation of the species because they are not nice and neat and tucked under between their legs. One of Granny's projects, whom she called "the poor soul," had a goiter. It was what might be called a goiter's goiter because it was as big as an orange. A few days after we had visited the lady with the goiter, a little boy dropped his pants in the schoolyard and showed me his equipment. I looked, assumed he was just another poor soul, and went home and asked Granny if we should take him some pea soup.

I skipped a year in elementary school, so all three of my adults felt that I was too young to date in high school. They ruled "No boys until college," but I did not really mind because I was too busy enjoying my adolescence. Growing up in Washington, D.C., was a delightful experience. The prewar Southernness lingered well into the fifties, lending life a leisurely pace, and the international aspect of the city provided me with a window on the larger world that Southerners do not generally have. My interests broadened, I discovered books, and became what is known as "sensitive."

Being an only child made things even nicer. I received a generous allowance and no instructions on how to spend it. I spent it on books. Every Saturday I would go down to Lowdermilk's secondhand store on G Street. I became a fixture and even received phone calls there. If I stayed too long, Granny would call the store and ask, "Is my granddaughter there? She buys Modern Library stories and chews her hair while she's reading." The manager never had any trouble finding me.

Gradually I got interested in sex in a calm, happy way. The first man in my life was Ivan Turgenev. I nearly had an orgasm when I read *On the Eve* and came to the scene in which Elena whispers "Take me" to Insarov. The curtain of charity closed abruptly after that line, but it was enough for me. I had no trouble imagining the pleasure Elena must have experienced because Insarov was literally feverish when they went to bed. He had TB, and Granny had often hinted that people with "consumption" are very highly sexed.

In my secret notebook, I copied down my favorite passage: *She sat down next to him and nestled close to him, and began to look at him with that laughing, tender and caressing glance that beams only in the eyes of a loving woman.* I translated it into French and then compared my version with that in a French edition. It wasn't bad at all—I forgot only one *passé simple*—and that thrilled me in another way because I wanted to be a French interpreter when I grew up. I had no thought of becoming a writer. I took six years of French and it filled my days with joy. I had my life planned: I would have my work and a wonderful sexy husband, also a linguist, and we would be a team like the Curies.

I was the happiest teenager in the world, but of course it could not last. In addition to my overweening hubris, I did not even have a pimple. Not one single pimple in my entire adolescence. The gods do not permit that kind of luck; so they sent me to college, where I learned at long last that it was a man's world.

2

"TOO MANY PARTIES AND TOO MANY PALS"
or My Four Years in a Penile Institution

My introduction to dormitory life was a bloodcurdling shriek of "Man in the hall!" For a split second utter silence reigned, then it was broken by peal after peal of the kind of hysterical giggles that mark sexually frustrated young females. Girls in petticoats and bath towels sprinted into hiding like terrified gazelles as somebody's cab driver came trudging up the stairs lugging a foot locker.

The girl in the room next door was sprawled across her bed, sobbing and planting kisses on a framed photograph, lurching up from time to time to moan, "I'll love him till I die!" Down the hall, Mario Lanza was singing "Be My Love" in competition with Kathryn Grayson and Howard Keel at the other end, in a sugary duet from *Show Boat*.

Behind me, I heard the simpering, cloying voice that can belong only to a 1950s roommate. She was reading aloud from a woman's magazine to a bevy of her friends: *"Even though I suffer excruciating cramps every month, I welcome my menstrual period because it proves that I'm a woman! I cherish all my female functions. I*

*just love being pregnant! We have four kids now, but I can't help it—I
want another baby!"*

"I want a whole houseful!" exclaimed one of the listeners. "It
can be done if you're scientific about it. Did you see Myrna Loy
in *Cheaper by the Dozen?"*

My roommate laid down the magazine, clasped her hands,
and closed her eyes reverently as she spoke.

"Having ... babies ... must ... be ... the ... most ...
wonderful ... experience ... in ... the ... *whole* ... world."

Then she turned to another article entitled, "We Put 'Obey'
Back in the Marriage Ceremony."

It would have helped if I had known that twenty years later, I
would be writing for that same magazine for top prices, but I
did not know. I was terrified as I stood in the door listening to
the din. All I knew was that something was terribly wrong, that
the integrated personality and special happiness I had known
were due to crumble. My instincts told me that I was out of my
element and threatened by something that had no name. Nowadays, it does have a name. Despite the overwhelming female
atmosphere of the dorm, I was knee-deep in male chauvinism.

Something told me to flee. In that moment, I almost quit
college on my first day. My feet moved forward, then back,
then forward again, until I was doing a kind of cakewalk there
in the hall by myself. Had it not been for the scholarship I had
won, I would have left. But I could not throw over a full-tuition
grant. Knowing that I was trapped, I started to cry.

A girl came by with an armful of men's socks. I later found
out that she washed them for her steady in the name of what
were then called "togetherness" and "preparation for marriage." It was one of the gamey items that went with love and
marriage, like a horse and carriage.

She put her arm around me and patted my shoulder.

"Did you break up with your boyfriend? Don't cry. Someday
you'll find somebody, and everything will be just wonderful."

She thrust out her chest so that I would be sure to see the fraternity pin that was affixed perilously close to her left nipple, almost hanging off the point. There was nothing smugger in the fifties than a girl who was engaged to be engaged.

She walked off singing "Three Little Words," while down the hall a group of giggly coeds burst into another song.

> *Though he ripped it and tore it*
> *I'm damn glad I wore it*
> *My sweet little Alice Blue Gown!*

The first gulf between the sexes that college presented me with was a literal one. The freshman picnic was held in a place known as The Grove, which contained an outdoor theater. The boys sat on one side of the stage and the girls on the other, while everyone sang "Roll Me Over, Lay Me Down, and Do It Again." When some of the boys started singing "Barnacle Bill the Sailor," the president of a sorority waved her hands frantically and cried, "The party's getting rough!" whereupon the president of the Inter-Fraternity Council turned his lantern jaw on the perpetrators and chided in clean-out Pat Boone tones: "Knock it off, men, there're ladies present."

The sorority president explained, "It's not that I'm a party poop. I *like* things that are *cute*, but I draw the line at *dirty*."

After defining her principles, she gathered us around her and recited the offending song, which contained the line: "It's only a pole to stick in your hole, said Barnacle Bill the Sailor." Someone said, "Oh, honestly!" in shocked tones, and the president nodded with approval.

"Boys like a girl with a good sense of humor, but if you let them go too far, they'll stop respecting you, and that's *it*." She drew her finger across her throat.

Being respected obsessed everyone. Any girl who was not respected had only herself to blame, people said. It was her fault if a boy "went too far" because it was up to her to "set the pace." Whole sororities lived in perpetual dread that one of their number would fall from grace, thereby imperiling the reputation of her sisters—"Everything you do reflects on us *all,*" our pledge mistress warned us.

It made no sense to me. In Granny's songs, everything was always the man's fault; now, it was the woman who was the villain of the piece. *He* was more to be pitied than censured because *she* was a cad.

My first dates were with boys in our "brother fraternity," Gamma Phi Upsilon (GPU). I did not particularly like any of them, but I wanted sex. My dreamy, dateless high school days had readied me, and now I was overdue. I did not, as yet, want to go to bed because that was unthinkable, but I wanted to experience what was called Everything But.

All I wanted was sex. I did not want the coffee shop flirtations, sock hops, frat parties, sorority sweetheart songs, hayrides, and proms, but it was the fifties, so I had to endure them because they were vital preliminaries in that mad ballet known as "making out." There were ground rules that had to be followed.

With a talent for partitioning unrivaled since the Congress of Vienna, the fifties coed divided herself into a rigidly classified set of love-play areas known as Above the Waist, Below the Waist, There, and that ultimate form of petting called Inside Me. To make matters even more complicated, there were the subcategories of Over the Clothes, Under the Clothes, Naked in the Front Seat, and Naked in the Back Seat.

This was the only means possible for so-called nice girls to satisfy curiosity, desire, and social convention all in one fell swoop. However, it had to be approached in a carefully graduated fashion; woe be to the girl who skipped a step, did everything at once, or did any of it with too many different boys. The GPUs kept a list of tramps in the same file with the used term papers.

French-kissing was no big deal; everybody did that except Kathleen Hanrahan, who used to kiss Pat Gilhooly through a handkerchief. The first real pas de deux that had to be negotiated was Above the Waist/Over the Clothes. My first venture into this field occurred with a boy who asked me for a date as we bent over the formaldehyde vat in zoology lab to fish out our fetal pigs.

In keeping with the ground rules, I had to wait three dates—a total of three weeks—before I could get my bust fondled. I could not even permit a kiss on the first date; on the second I was able to allow a dry one, and on the third date it was okay to neck in the car, which included French-kissing. If the girl did not pull away, it was a signal that the boy could go further.

I had to wait an interminable time to get what I wanted. We French-kissed through "O Mein Papa," "Hernando's Hideaway," and "The Barefoot Contessa" (the theme song from an Ava Gardner movie about a man without a penis).

Finally, he did it, but we might just as well have shaken hands because I didn't feel a thing. Besides a taffeta dress and a camisole slip, I was wearing a bra with circular-stitched cups to achieve that collie-muzzle point so popular in the fifties, and it was lined to make sure that the outline of the nipples was hidden.

The next day in zoology class he was strangely silent. Finally, he looked at me over the pig and spoke in a sorrowful voice.

"Look, I don't think we better see each other again. I'm afraid you're getting too serious. See, I'm going to be a doctor, and I can't afford to get serious for a long time. Gotta crack the books, you know? Ha-ha. And . . . well, I know you're getting serious about me."

"Serious? About you?" I said.

He did not catch my inflection.

"Yes, I'm afraid so," he sighed. He blushed furiously and went on. "A girl doesn't let a guy do . . . *that* to her unless she's in love with him."

He put his hand on my shoulder and smiled in that tight-lipped, chin-clenching Charlton Heston style. "But I want you to know that I still respect you. A lot of guys wouldn't, but I do. You're a wonderful person, and you'll find somebody to love you someday—and he'll be one lucky guy!"

Never before or since have I been so nonplused. I was verbally hors de combat. How could I tell him that I was simply using him to find out what it felt like to have my bust fondled? I stood there with my mouth open as he walked off.

I will say one thing for him: he kept *his* mouth shut. He did not tell the GPU on me; so I pressed on in Above the Waist/ Over the Clothes with another boy. I took care to wear something a little more suited to such abandoned intimacy, but even my most wanton bra had enough lace to outfit the Pope for Easter Sunday High Mass; so I switched to Above the Waist/ Under the Clothes.

According to sorority ground rules, this practice had to be initiated on a special occasion, a big date such as a semiformal frat party. In a mood of cynical premeditation, I wore a strapless bra that I could simply unhook and toss aside. However, since it was a semiformal affair, I had to wear a cocktail dress, and since it was 1954, all my cocktail dresses had halter necklines.

That was the night I almost hanged myself. My date, Pete, had been rubbing my bare back long enough to discover the zipper in my dress. He lowered the tab, and I made ready to slip the yoke over my head, which would have allowed the dress to fall conveniently off the entire top half of me. I had my head halfway through the halter when Pete, overcome with sudden lust, seized my bra and, instead of unhooking it, followed my example and yanked it up around my neck in an attempt to pull it over my head. The bra caught me under the chin, the dress got stuck in my earrings, and my sorority pin came undone and pierced my nose.

Pete tried to remedy matters by twisting the bra to free it—a solution akin to using the albatross as a tourniquet. I ended up jackknifed forward, tossing and jerking my head like a horse in a martingale.

Pete leaned over and said, "Are you all right?" at which precise moment, the car door opened and I had the first of my many compromising encounters with Matthew X. Kearny, the campus warden.

Kearny was a retired cop who roamed around looking for cars without any heads in them. He would let you alone if he could see two heads, more or less side by side in the front seat. If you slid down below window level, or if he saw you in the back, he would yank open the door, shine his foot-long flashlight in, and say, needlessly, "What's going on here?"

I felt a blast of cold air; then the car was flooded with light, and Kearny's gravelly voice started barking out questions.

"What's going on here? What're you kids up to? What in the hell is wrong with *her?*"

"She . . . had an accident," Pete mumbled.

"Sit up, girlie!" Kearny ordered and tapped me on my bare back with his icy flashlight. I gurgled out a yell.

"I can't move!"

"What didya do to her, buddy?"

"I didn't do anything," Pete said in a quavering voice. "She must have pulled a muscle."

"Yeah? A muscle in her *what?* Look here, girlie, you can't stay like that all night. Where do you live? Start the car, buddy, I'm escortin' the two of you back to her dorm."

Kearny drove at a menacingly slow speed, like the Irish Guards' Last Post for cavalry funerals. We followed him to my dorm. I finally got my bra unhooked and my head free just as we pulled up to the front door. There was just time enough to duck, braless, back into the halter and zip up the dress before Kearny opened my door and led me up the steps. The bra was so full of wires that I could not fold it and hide it in either my purse or my pocket; so I carried it.

Kearny glanced grimly at it, shook his head, and gave me some avuncular advice.

"Listen, girlie, it takes years to build up a good reputation, but only a minute to tear it down. There's a song that was popular back in the days when I was a sport. 'These Broadway roses and frivolous Sals had too many parties and too many pals.'"

"Oh, no," I moaned.

Kearny held up a stubby warning finger. "There's a lot of truth in them old songs, girlie. Remember these sports are out for all they can get, but when the time comes for them to choose the mother of their children, they're not gonna want damaged goods. Oh, they'll feed you a good line all right, I did the same thing when I was a sport, but you know somethin'? I was just testin' 'em, I really wanted 'em to say no, in my heart of hearts. 'Cause I was lookin' for a *good* girl, see? Now you take my advice: when these sports say, 'If you love me, you will,' you just tell 'em old Kearny's answer: 'If you love him, you *won't*.' Now you wanna stay as sweet as you are, you don't wanna be no soiled dove. So you go on in now and get your beauty sleep and be a good girl from now on."

I didn't wanna be no soiled dove, but I did want my bosom played with. The next time I went out I wore a cardigan sweater and actually contemplated going without a bra, but of course I did not dare, so I wore a strapless. My GPU on this night was named Wade and, *mirabile dictu*, nothing bizarre happened. He unbuttoned my sweater, unhooked my bra with a mere flick of his wrist, and began. I not only got my bosom played with, I got it nibbled—known in the fifties as "He kissed me up top."

This was more like it. I was so busy enjoying myself that I completely forgot about keeping our heads above window level. I slid down in the seat, and Wade, attached like a leech, slid down with me.

Suddenly the door burst open.

"All right, you kids, straighten up and fly right. Start that motor, buddy, I'm escortin' you back to the dorm."

We drove to the dorm, and Kearny beckoned me to follow him up the steps. At the door he sighed, shook his head, and settled his Celtic Agrippa features into stern lines.

"My wife, rest her soul, gave me three fine daughters. They're all married now, thanks be to God, and they got a fine bunch of children, so I know what I'm talkin' about, right? You wanna be left on the shelf? You wanna be the last rose of summer, dyin' on the stem?"

" 'Left blooming alone,' " I corrected.

"That's what I said. You wanna end up one of them hard, shopworn dames? When a sport looks for a wife, he wants a girl that's soft and sweet."

"I'm soft and sweet," I said, as I stuffed my bra in my coat pocket.

"I mean in your heart of hearts," Kearny replied, blushing. "If you let these sports make free with you, you'll be ever a bridesmaid and never a bride. Now I'm not gonna tell you again. I want you to go upstairs and say your prayers to the Blessed Mother."

"That's a Romish error," I said, quoting the Book of Common Prayer.

"Never mind," said Kearny. "You need all the help you can get."

When I got upstairs, I showered, got ready for bed, and opened my American Literature textbook. By now, the sexual tension and battleground atmosphere of college had destroyed my former erudition. I still got good grades, but I was not learning anything. Only an ability to read fast and a near-photographic memory kept me on the dean's list.

I had heard all the whispers about those male problems known as "blue balls" or "lover's nuts," but there was no name for the comparable pain that women feel because officially, women were not supposed to feel it. Having grown up in a Southern gynecocracy full of dramatic tales of tilted wombs and the change of life, I could not imagine a male illness that a woman could not top. But there I was with an unrecognized malady. I could feel my vagina stretching into an awareness of itself; it felt long, wide, and empty.

I opened to the next day's assignment, exquisitely titled *The Turn of the Screw*, and stared down at a sentence that was even more turgid than my loins.

> It took of course more than that particular passage to place us together in presence of what we had now to live with as we could—my dreadful liability to impressions of the order so vividly exemplified, and my companion's knowledge, henceforth,—a knowledge half consternation and half compassion,—of that liability.

Try reading Henry James when you're horny, just try it.

Below the Waist/There, or intimate digitation, was serious business reserved for a boy you were practically going steady with. It was considered a properly improper way to round off a really special date such as a formal dance. Consequently, you both almost smothered to death because yards and yards of material came flying up in your face: flounced tulle, linings (everything was lined), underskirts, petticoats, crinolines, and a six-tier steel hoop. These were ultrafeminine times.

When you finally got your pudenda excavated, the next problem was negotiating a garment known as a Merry Widow, which simply could not be removed. It was a combination half-cup strapless bra, waist-pincher, girdle, garter belt, and pants, all in one. It was made of lace over satin over starched canvas, and reinforced with fifteen strips of steel. It amputated the wearer at the hip, left deep red welts, cut off circulation in the legs, and threatened spontaneous clitorodectomy because it had a detachable crotch piece that tended to ride up. However, the crotch piece was very convenient for heavy petting because all one needed to do was unsnap four snaps and *voilà*.

Some of the boys knew about the clitoris and some did not, but even the most enlightened sports left much to be desired. They were so used to masturbating themselves in hearty male fashion that the result was more often pain than pleasure. One boy actually started slapping me with his palm.

Wade was one of the better ones, however. I went to the prom with him, and afterward we went out to the car, where I unsnapped my crotch piece, tossed it on the dash, and had at it.

Once the game was afoot, I had to concentrate on trying to keep his finger in the right place while we both kept one eye peeled for Kearny and recited the deathless dialogue that always accompanied these diddling sessions.

"Here?"

"Higher."

"There?"

"Lighter."

"Like this?"

"Further up top."

"Does that feel good?"

"Lower!"

"Where is it?"

"There!"

"More?"

"Slower."

"Like that?"

"Oh, there!"

"Do you like that?"

"Oh, don't stop!"

"I think I hear Kearny."

A girl wearing four-inch spike heels and having an orgasm in the front seat of a car can do a great deal of damage. There were a lot of broken heaters. One of my sorority sisters stripped the gears and another put her foot through the windshield, but it fell to me to become a campus legend.

Wade found the right place and I had an orgasm. My feet flew up and somehow, some way, my heel got caught in the horn rim. The horn blasted away, and as I struggled to free myself I pressed the rim harder and the horn stuck. I panicked at the noise and twisted my ankle under the steering wheel in an effort to get untangled, and a numbing pain shot up my leg. I yelled and buried Wade under a cascade of tulle, petticoats, and crinoline. By now I was practically standing on my head and my legs were spread out as far as they would reach.

The noise brought Kearny out of the bulrushes with his flashlight at charge. He yanked open the door, rammed the flashlight in the car, and hit me right on the bare crotch.

"What's goin' on here?"

"The horn's stuck!" Wade yelled.

"*I'm* stuck!"

Kearny ran to the hood, threw it open, and yanked at the wires. The horn cut off, but I was still paralyzed. Kearny peered in, then quickly turned his back.

"Cover yourself, girlie."

By twisting out of my shoe, rolling over onto my stomach, and doing a kind of swimming stroke, I got free and sat up.

Kearny turned around.

"Oh, no, it's you again," he muttered. He stuck his flashlight in his belt and jerked his thumb in the direction of my dorm.

As Kearny escorted me up the dorm steps, my leg kept giving way and thrusting me into a series of genuflections that I hoped would please him. When we got to the door he pushed his cap back over his curly gray hair and shook his head.

"What kinda hothouse flower are you tryin' to be? You gonna end up in a home, you know that? They got places for girls like you. If you was my daughter, I'd throw you outta the house for good!"

That did it. I opened my mouth and let him have it:

She held the baby to her breast
And wept sad tears of shame.
With footsteps slow and no place to go,
She walked through the snow in vain.

The next day, I was campused for a month for being drunk and singing on the dorm steps at one in the morning.

I spent my house arrest brooding. I was sick of the Richie Cunninghams who populated my unhappy days. They were like a gestapo in white sports coats, vigilant in the cause of finding, "testing," and punishing "dirty girls." The Furies and the Fates were supposed to be female but now they had become male.

For a while I considered becoming the mistress of an older, exotic man. It would have been so easy to manage in Washington with all the diplomats around. Every time I walked down Massachusetts Avenue someone in a turban would stick his head out of a black limousine, roll his eyes like marbles, and say "Ahhhh!" I was the physical type that Levantine voluptuaries crave. I wanted to take one to a sorority dance just for the pleasure of hearing Kearny say "Jay-sus!"

I decided that boys had sex *on* their minds but not *in* their minds. Mental sex—as opposed to fantasies—was foreign to them. I wanted to combine lovemaking and mind-making, but I found no one with whom I could exchange interior passionate awareness. It had nothing to do with intellect per se, for the most intelligent boys on campus were the most disappointing. These were the science majors, the boys with soaring IQs who wore leather-encased slide rules on their belts—the Excalibur of the twentieth century, slapping against gray flannel. They refused to read *Daniel Deronda* because they considered it a waste of their time, so they borrowed my notes. Thus when I necked with them, I was, in a sense, necking with myself.

I began to suspect that boys were not so highly sexed as they pretended to be. They used the myth of eternal tumescence for a variety of reasons. It was very convenient for fleeing a girl who was too responsive, as in: "If I stay any longer, I won't be responsible for what happens." It was also convenient for explaining the better grades that girls got, as in: "You can concentrate better because you're not a slave to your body."

I decided that females have sexual desire. Males simply have sexual tension.

I spent the remainder of my house arrest looking for my hymen. It was a popular pastime in the fifties. Every time a girl indulged in Below the Waist/There, she locked herself in the bathroom with a hand mirror to see if her pearl beyond price was still intact.

I took a mirror and a flashlight and settled down in a stall in the john. I didn't really know what a hymen looked like, but I pictured it as a kind of veil or shield. I had shields on the brain because Granny, who was determined to prove her descent from royalty, had acquired a copy of Burke's *Peerage*. I probed carefully for something *engoulé gardant* but I could find nothing sufficiently steely and unequivocal. I had in mind something like a trapdoor *entée en point*, but all I could find were lips *flanchées*, urethra *cleché*, and, naturally, after all that diddling around, a clitoris *rampant*.

As I leaned back to get a better look, I lost my balance and dropped the flashlight in the toilet. I leaped up and stared at it in terror, expecting it to explode. I didn't dare reach in and get it because I was afraid I'd be electrocuted. The difference between electricity and batteries meant nothing to me; all I knew was that a light was a light, and if you touched it with wet hands you would go up in smoke.

After a few minutes of numb helplessness, I remembered that current is broken by rubber so I ran back to my room for my rain boots. I had no rubber gloves, so I put one boot on my right foot and slipped the other on my hand. Clad in nothing but a slip, I hopped to the bathroom, fished the flashlight out with my makeshift glove, and hopped back down the hall toward my room with a dripping flashlight in my booted hand just in time to meet the dean of women.

"It's science," I babbled. "A scientific experiment. Homework." Before she could say anything I hopped into my room and locked the door.

Living in constant fear that we had broken our hymens and ruined ourselves for marriage produced in the fifties coed a masochistic compulsion to try Tampax. It was sheer self-flagellation: we had to punish ourselves for heavy petting by ramming a Tampax all the way home. That way, we could blame the loss of our hymens on Tampax instead of heavy petting. It made no sense, but we were all half-mad by this time.

I bought a box of Regular and a jar of Vaseline and locked myself in a bathroom stall while several of my sorority sisters stood outside the door shouting encouragement and reading aloud the instructions in the brochure.

"It says you're supposed to push it toward the small of your back!"

"Squat! It says to squat!"

"I'm squatting! Oh, God . . ."

I used up the whole box trying. The next day, I finally managed to plant a Junior. The whole area felt as though it were on fire, like the hands and feet of a saint who has just received his stigmata. A wave of nausea swept me as I thought, *I'm not a virgin anymore.* I wondered if I had bled, but there was no way to tell since I was already menstruating. It was too confusing to bear. I rose, turned around, and threw up.

Now there were no barriers to the practice of Inside Me. I went out with Wade and after about twenty minutes of the lesser stuff, he speared me. Naturally there was another death-less dialogue.

"Am I hurting you?"

"No!"

glick-blick-slook.

"Do you want me to use two fingers?"

"Yes!"

glick-blick-slook.

"Harder!"

"My arm hurts."

"Give it to me!"

glick-blick-slook.

The next day I had a lit exam. The first question was: "Define onomatopoeia."

Satisfying the boys was something we did with the utmost reluctance because we were all scared to death of semen. If it got *on* you, anywhere *near* you, you *could* get pregnant, it *had* happened. A sheaf of horror stories made the rounds of the sorority, all about girls who had gotten pregnant ("P.G.") in swimming pools because a boy had ejaculated nearby, and one chilling tale about the New York water shortage and the girl who, in a spirit of civic responsibility, had used her brother's bathwater after him. Somebody was always cutting out one of those first-person confessions about girls who "fooled around," which we called Playing On But Not In. We cranked ourselves up into such a state of terror that we visualized each individual sperm cell as a grinning demon armed with pontoons, ladders, scaling hooks, wire cutters, and an ability to incubate indef-initely in everything from wool to nylon tricot to Ship 'n' Shore blouses.

So we satisfied the boys by letting them rub against us with their flies closed. In the frat house we let them get on top of us, but in cars it was done side by side. To be safe, we always put our pants back on and pulled our skirts back down. When the boys started to ejaculate we screamed, "Don't let it get on me!" and pulled away with all our strength.

The man who ran the dry cleaning shop drove a Cadillac.

Sometimes the boys managed to get their flies open in time to finish on the floor while we plastered ourselves against the door and pulled our feet out of the way—sperm cells, we had read, swam upward, and we were certain that a single sperm could splash valiantly all the way up a girl's leg, dive under the elastic band of her underpants, and GET IN ME. One of my sorority sisters was scared silly of even being *in* the car during an ejaculation. One night she ran all the way up to the gym to flee the encroaching semen.

Though none of us had had intercourse, we were always certain we were pregnant. Math majors sat in calculus class counting up their "late" days on their fingers while boys and professors stared in consternation and wondered what the *hell* they were doing. We huddled in fearful knots in the sorority suite and asked each other peculiar questions with an air of panicky intensity, like: "What day was it that your mother bought you that green sack dress that you hated and traded to Ginny for the black suede heels? For God's sake, you've *got* to remember!"

Although everyone knew that nice girls simply did not go all the way, once in a while a boy would plead for the final favor anyway. One night I almost yielded to Joe Simpson.

"Please!" he begged.

I stopped fiddling with him and started counting on my fingers. I was certain that I had gotten the curse the day after I turned in the term paper on the War of Jenkins' Ear, but I couldn't remember when that was. All I knew was that I had been sitting in the sorority suite making up footnotes for the quotations I had invented when Kathleen Hanrahan rushed in screaming that somebody would have to drive her to Confession right away because she had just French-kissed with Pat Gilhooly, and if she happened to die in the middle of the night she'd go to hell.

Which must have been Pat's birthday because Kathleen had been wondering what to give him and we had all recommended a real kiss for a change instead of her usual handkerchief number that the nuns had recommended. So my period must have started two days after that.

"Let's get in the back!" Joe panted.

"When is Pat Gilhooly's birthday?"

"What!"

"I'm afraid I'm in my middle now even though it's three days earlier than my usual middle because last month was February, which always messes everything up because it's so short."

"Huh?"

The scientific age, which so erodes male sex appeal, had peaked, so Joe whispered hotly: "Statistics show that it's scientifically impossible for a girl to get P.G. the first time she does it. I read this book. There's a one-in-ten-million chance that anything'll happen." This is the American man's version of the sweet nothing. I probably would have come across if he had said something romantic or desperate; at that stage of my novel-reading, I would have considered a suicide threat irresistibly Hungarian. But being told that a girl can't get P.G. because the Trojan Prophylactic Company runs a test kitchen was guaranteed to keep me pure.

I finally masturbated a boy while I was sloshed to the gills at a formal dance during my senior year. It was an almost impossible task because I was wearing the requisite eighteen-inch white kid gloves that fit like skin. No one in the fifties would have dreamed of going to a formal dance without them. Once you got them on, which took twenty minutes per hand, you could not get them off again, but fortunately the designer had had the foresight to include six little pearl buttons on the insides of the wrists so that properly dressed ladies could withdraw their hands to drink, smoke, and—presumably—masturbate their dates at formal dances, which is how it came to pass that Kearny found me with the fingers of my right glove rolled back, swishing my hand around in the quadrangle fountain.

I did it not out of desire or even curiosity, but out of rebellion. I was sick of the sex rules, sick of divvying up the various portions of my person and worrying about above-this and below-that. It had become eerily like the Treaty of Versailles, with one of my breasts awarded to Greece and the other to Turkey, and access to my vagina weighed as if it were the Dardanelles. I got so fed up that I quit the sorority—not an easy thing to do because the secret ritual had been revealed to me, not to mention the handshake—and made up my mind to lose my virginity.

Or to be more precise, to have normal vaginal intercourse.

I arranged to sublet an apartment for the rest of the term, telling my parents, whose written permission I needed for the dean of women, that the dorm was too noisy for the great work I was embarked upon. (It was a term paper on the War of the Austrian Succession, which was caused by the War of Jenkins' Ear).

Next, I needed birth control. I took it for granted that all men used condoms, but I wanted an extra safeguard, so I decided to buy the only women's contraceptive that I knew about—vaginal suppositories.

It was a miracle that I knew about them because ads in those days were masterpieces of euphemism. They sounded like mothers. They always pictured a woman who looked as ladylike as Irene Dunne, and the copy read: ". . . to keep you dainty and feminine at all times. Destroys ALL unwanted germs in the most personal area of your body. You can be SAFE, sure, and confident that your womanly delicacy and fastidiousness will never desert you."

I strolled nonchalantly into the drugstore. As luck would have it, the clerk was young and male.

"I'd like a box of Norforms, please," I said casually.

"What size?"

I stared at him in horror. How was I supposed to know what size my vagina was? For a moment I contemplated running out of the store, then I reasoned that since I wore Junior Tampax, I would take a Junior Norform.

"Small," I said firmly.

He brought out a tiny box.

"Oh, that's not enough!" I blurted, thinking of the orgy I had planned.

"You want the large economy size?" he asked, and produced it.

The light dawned. "Oh, you mean *that* kind of size!"

"That's right," he said, grinning harder. "The box."

I wanted to die.

Somehow I got back to campus. Remembering my difficulties with Tampax, I decided to "wear" a suppository to make sure I was used to them before the Big Moment, so I popped a Norform and went off to my class in seventeenth-century French drama. We were translating *Phèdre* and the professor called on me to read. I stood up and began.

> *O toi, qui vois la honte où je suis descendue,*
> *Implacable Vénus, suis-je assez confondue?*
> *Tu ne saurais plus loin—*

I broke off suddenly as a warm inundation drenched the seat of my pants. Something started running down my leg. I crossed one thigh over the other and stood there in utter terror.

"What does that mean?" asked the professor.

There was another gush as I began to translate.

"You, implacable Venus, who see the shame to which I have fallen, am I not brought low enough?"

The Big Moment arrived. It seemed strange not having a door handle sticking in my back. I used three Norforms, just to be sure, and to be absolutely sure, I decided to take a douche afterward. I ended up baptizing myself with two quarts of warm water generously spiked with Zonite when the nail on the back of the bathroom door popped out of the wood and my douche bag went splat.

Naturally, I panicked. If by some infinitesimal chance a single intrepid sperm cell had managed not to be trapped, smothered, poisoned, or simply discouraged, it would still be in me and I would get P.G. unless I prepared another douche. So I did. I filled the bag and stood there holding it as I looked wildly around, wondering what in the hell to do with it. There was no place to hang it.

I thought about hammering the nail back in the door, but the hammer was in the kitchen. Could I rush stark naked past my lover holding a full douche bag, and then rush back again brandishing a hammer? I thought not. I had heard about women who took douches in the bathtub with the bag hung on the shower nozzle, but the ancient flat I had sublet had no shower, just a tub. There was nothing to do but sit on the john and hold the bag high over my head with my left hand while I performed the ablutions with my right.

As I said earlier, this was the Togetherness era. I am not the Togetherness type, but my lover, a friendly sort, was. He stalked into the bathroom as boldly as Charlotte Corday, a knotted rubber in his hand, and there I was like a pornographic Statue of Liberty, lifting my douche bag beside the plywood door.

3

THE SPERM AND I
or Planned Nonparenthood
Before the Pill

Nothing brings out the full bloom of the battle of the sexes like birth control. Nowadays the problem is about as unobtrusive as we can make it. Contraceptives are in the bloodstream or floating around in the uterus, never to be touched by the human hand. Men get vasectomies and even wear ruptured-duct lapel pins like war veterans. Lovers can now find condoms advertised in magazines. Clip the coupon and you can get a year's supply in decorator colors and a personalized carrying case.

It was not always thus. I was there on Crispin's Day when condoms were manufactured "for the prevention of disease."

Nowadays condoms are actually called condoms. In fifties girl-talk sessions they were called "those rubber things." Men generally called them by their brand names when they bought them, and referred to them in jokes and bull sessions as "socks" and "pros." I observed that Northern men called them "safes" while Southern men called them "raincoats." This says some interesting things about the wide variety of American habits. It also says some interesting things about the wide variety of my habits.

In mixed company, condoms had no name at all, but that didn't stop us from talking about them constantly. Sex in the fifties was a land of hope and Something.

"Do you have something?"

"Do I need something?"

"Don't worry, I've got something."

"If I use something, will you take it in your mouth?"

Condoms were sold in whispers, and in vending machines in the men's room of Southern gas stations. The Southern lover pulled into a gas station and bought his condoms from the men's room machine. Then he would stop by the bubble gum machine and put a coin in that, then the peanut machine, then the candy machine, and finally the pinball machine. The foremost sound in the South is *ding!* Southern men love slots.

When I went to graduate school at Ole Miss in 1958, I didn't know about the men's room vending machines until a man told me. I refused to believe it at first, until he bet me a dollar I was wrong, which is how I came to be caught in the men's room of a Natchez gas station by a state trooper answering a call of nature. I played dumb and pretended I had opened the wrong door, and of course he believed me. He even apologized for startling me, and manfully insisted that it was all his fault. There was a great deal of ma'am-ing and hat-tipping. By the time it was all over, I felt as magnanimous as Granny on a charity run. Southern men are wonderful; they always Play the Game.

All men used condoms, but they hated them; so there was an ever-present temptation not to bother using them. This always resulted in a running argument that seemed to go on forever. Men tried every ploy. A favorite was, "Let's start out without one, and I'll stop and put one on just before I come." This is on a par with other famous male promises, like: "Just give me the Sudetenland, and I'll stop."

If a man were planning to make a night of it, he always

carried a whole box of condoms. At other times—i.e., every day—he carried a single condom, wrapped in tinfoil, in his wallet because he never knew when a girl might just come across. One night in a parked car on a popular thoroughfare near Ole Miss called the "Hard Road" (because it was paved), I decided to come across. The night was pitch-black and the windows were so steamed up that we couldn't see a thing. My beau reached into his wallet, pulled something out, and tore it down the middle. It was his Social Security card.

Men loved to orchestrate the use of a condom. Before applying one, the fifties man used to blow it up to test it for holes. When he had his balloon nice and fat, he held it up to his lady friend and said, "See?" Afterward, he held it up again to prove that it had not sprung a leak. "See?" A used condom is not an ennobling sight to a woman, but a man loves to gaze upon his collected semen. That's *him* in there, and looking at it is a supreme ego trip. At such moments he thinks about how many millions of little hims that inch or so of fluid could create, so he is in no hurry to dispose of it. Eventually he got up and took it into the john, where, instead of flushing it away, he stalled some more. This was the third test of the condom's strength. He ran water into it to make another, heavier balloon, then brought it back to the bedroom. "See?" he said proudly, holding it aloft. By this time the poor little condom couldn't take any more; it burst, splashing water and millions of little hims all over the proud tester's bare feet.

Pantyhose have done much to put a stop to men's interest in dressing and undressing a woman. The only man who could get a woman into or out of a pair of pantyhose is an undertaker. In the stocking era, men loved to help a woman on and off with her leg wear. They handled stockings as if they were condoms. When a man took a stocking off, he took hold of the toe and yanked. When they put a stocking on you, they always left a little room in the toe and then carefully rolled ... rolled ... rolled their way up to mid-thigh.

As a quid pro quo, they liked to have a woman put their condoms on for them. The first time I applied a condom I did it the way I would put on my stockings. I slipped the end neatly around the head of the penis, then I pulled tautly so that it would be nice and snug and wouldn't bag. Guess what happened? It broke. Guess where? Guess when? Guess what didn't happen? I didn't get P.G. There must have been an angel sitting on my cervix because it was the fifteenth day of my cycle.

An even worse condom experience occurred when a man used one that was made not of rubber but of some esoteric and very expensive substance—the pleuroperitoneum of an aborted lamb or something like that. I gathered that it was the dernier cri of status symbols even though it had a repulsive-looking lubricated tip that reminded me of a misplaced nipple. I don't know what sort of lubricating fluid it contained, but I have a feeling it was glue.

The man who used it was very proud of his genital size. Every time we finished making love he always winced theatrically and said, "These damn safes always choke me," and then peeled it off with overdone grimaces of pain. The night he used the lamb-gut condom, he went through the same proud performance. "This damn thing chokes me, too. Have to take it off."

He reached down, and suddenly his proud grin vanished.

"It *is* off."

He started patting the bed. I started patting the bed.

"Lift up your butt," he ordered, but it was not there, either.

He tossed back the sheet. "I wonder where it could—" he began, and then stopped. We stared at each other. I found it *in situ*, but I didn't get P.G. that time, either.

I discovered vaginal jelly. It is a colorless and extremely slick spermacide that must be applied with a plunger-type applicator. One was supposed to buy the jelly-with-applicator kit the first time, *keep* the applicator, and thereafter buy only the jelly. It was a lovely thought. It infused unladylike behavior with a good dose of old-fashioned, all-American thrift, but like most lovely thoughts it didn't work. I left a trail of forgotten applicators in tourist cabins from one end of the Natchez Trace to the other, and in just about every hotel in Memphis.

The applicator tube contains two lines. The first one, an inch or so up from the tip, marks the amount of jelly to be used with a diaphragm. The second line, five inches up from the tip, marks the amount to be used if you intend to perform without a diaphragm. I had no diaphragm as yet, so I was concerned with the second line. However, I was terrified of getting P.G., so "just to be sure," as we said in the fifties, I used two tubefuls.

Ten inches of vaginal jelly can do wonders for a woman's reputation. "God," he breathed. "You're wonderful ... so highly sexed. I never felt anything like it. You're really wet!"

My mistakes seldom turn out so well. My next experience with vaginal jelly was more in character. I was living in a dorm again so I had to do my sinning in motels, which meant I had to tote a tube of vaginal jelly wherever I went. I simply tossed it in my handbag, where, being a student, I also kept lots of pens and pencils with sharp points.

As we were driving to the motel, my beau discovered that he was out of cigarettes, so he reached into my bag for one of mine—and drove off the road straight into a cornfield.

There was vaginal jelly smeared and oozing all over my bag. My beau, a Korean War combat veteran, was staring in horror at his hand and muttering, "My God, it felt like reaching into somebody's insides."

The state troopers came, inspected the demolished fence, sniffed our breaths, and asked to see my university I.D. When I handed the trooper my card, he wrinkled his nose and bared his teeth.

"Wus' all this here gunk? Where y'all been, down in the sewer?"

"I spilled some hand lotion in my bag," I said weakly.

After it was all over, I had to listen to a War Story which went on forever and finally ended with: "... so that's why I lost control of the car. It brought it all back to me. Like I say, it felt just like reaching into somebody's insides."

The time had come to get a diaphragm. It was not easy to do in the fifties. I had to lie and say I was going to be married the following month before the doctor would agree to fit me. Since I was twenty-one and single, he assumed that I would take a 65, but when he inserted the ring, it practically floated away. After a few more tries, he found that I took an 80. Apparently I have terminal *ultima Thule.* The doctor exploded in fury, shouting, "That's a married woman's size!" and accused me of leading an immoral life. He refused to write a prescription for me, and ordered me out of his office. (As *MS.* magazine correctly observed, every woman has a gynecologist story.) I finally found a woman doctor in a seedy downtown hotel who prescribed what I needed without comment.

Now that I had a diaphragm, my biggest problem was how to let men know that I had one without letting them know that I had one. Men are ambivulent creatures; they were delighted to find out that you owned a diaphragm because it meant that they would not have to use condoms. On the other hand, they hated to think that you *already* had one. Each man wanted to think that you bought it *for him.*

Okay. If that's the way they wanted it, that's the way they got it. I bought a brand-new diaphragm that was an exact replica in every way of the one I already had. I kept it solely for purposes of show. Whenever I took up with a new man, I let him use condoms the first couple of times, then I would work the conversation around to better forms of birth control.

"I wish there were something I could do so you wouldn't have to use those rubber things. I know you don't like them."

"Did you ever think of getting a diaphragm?" he would ask.

"Oh . . . I've heard of them. What exactly are they? How do you get one?"

Godlike, he explained, and humbly, I listened. A few days later I would take my untouched decoy diaphragm from its hiding place and show it to my new man.

"I did what you said and went to the doctor. This is what he gave me."

Propriety was so strong in those days that the brochure that accompanied the diaphragm always showed a dainty hand wearing a gold wedding band in the instruction pictures. Thus an overwhelming number of right-handed women had to figure out how to insert a diaphragm from a left-handed illustration. The brochure also took care to point out: "You can store your diaphragm in its attractve plastic case without fear of embarrassment because it is especially designed to resemble a compact."

It certainly was. One night after three martinis in the cocktail lounge of a New Orleans hotel, I reached into my bag for my compact and started powdering my nose with a diaphragm before I realized what I was doing.

Diaphragms came with a plastic inserter for women who had aesthetic objections to touching themselves *there*. The inserter also enabled the user to avoid pop flies. Squeezing a jelly-smeared diaphragm into a figure eight is dangerous business. I never bothered with the inserter. If I had used one I could have avoided a dreadful night.

As I have pointed out, this was the Togetherness era, and its ramifications were endless, cretinous, and occasionally revolting. Foremost among the latter was that piece of advice that fifties sex manuals came up with: "Keep your diaphragm beside the bed so you will not have to interrupt the glow of romance once you and your husband begin to make love."

Inserting a diaphragm in front of a man is enough to make him turn queer on the spot. I didn't want to do it, but he pleaded and I gave in. We were lying in bed in the glow of the lamp and I was smearing jelly on the diaphragm. When it was ready, I pinched it in half and prepared to insert it when suddenly it went *flick!* up in the air and landed across the room, practically between the paws of my cat. She woke up and pounced. A nude chase scene ensued, with me trilling, "Come to Mommy." My lover suggested distracting her with some other article and swapping it for the diaphragm. I tried her toy mouse, and then a yo-yo—standing in the middle of the living room stark naked, playing with a yo-yo—all to no avail. No human ever wins these skirmishes; cats invented psychology. She crawled under a cabinet and happily sank her claws in my diaphragm. By that time so much dust had stuck to it that she probably thought it was a mouse—the next day she emerged with the shredded remains in her mouth and dropped it at my feet.

I didn't want to consult the vet on such a delicate matter, but I had to. I was afraid she might have poisoned herself with vaginal jelly.

"My cat may have swallowed some vaginal jelly."

"Oh? How did that happen?"

"She may have licked it off my diaphragm." The *mays* helped me to suggest that perhaps the whole ungodly mess had never occurred.

As things turned out, she was all right—and I ended up having an affair with the vet. He was the only man I didn't have to play my diaphragm trick on.

The diaphragm was the bane of women with long fingernails because it was so easy to puncture, but I have always kept my nails short, so that, at least, was never a problem. I destroyed several diaphragms in a much more colorful way.

I always lived alone, so I got accustomed to leaving personal items sitting out in full view in my bathroom. After a diaphragm is removed, it must be washed and propped up to dry on a wad of paper. In several of my apartments, the bathroom radiator was beside the john, so I forgot and put the diaphragms there. I never realized what had happened until I smelled the stench of burning rubber.

The best place to burn up your diaphragms is Mississippi because it is so easy to replace them. In the fifties, you could buy anything in Mississippi except whiskey. A girl I knew at the university used to buy amphetamines by the Mason jar. The reason for Mississippi's casual attitude toward selling diaphragms was not because it is an overwhelmingly Protestant state. It goes deeper into the souls of Mississippians than even that. On the box in which the diaphragm is sold there is a stern notation: "Federal law prohibits the sale of this article except with a doctor's prescription." The words *federal law* were enough for Mississippi. They would sell you diaphragms by the quire.

An old-fashioned but surprisingly successful method of birth control is one that I overheard Granny talking about once. It is a small sponge dipped in vinegar and used like a diaphragm. I tried it once after I had burned up my rubber diaphragm, and I didn't get P.G. There was only one problem: there was nothing in the house except garlic vinegar.

I took a complete chance only once in my life, or as Southern girls prefer to say, "I was swept off my feet and lost my head." It happened in a Mississippi woods on one of those scent-laden summer nights that seem to be Mississippi's trademark. The man I was with was the best lover I have ever had, and the sex was perfect, the "Yes, yes, oh, yes" Frank Yerby kind, complete with a vaginal orgasm. (Yes, Ms. Virginia, there is such a thing.) All in all, it would have shone in my memory as the most romantic night of my life, but for what happened afterward.

The quintessential Southern method of emergency contraception is a Coca-Cola douche. You take a bottle of warm Coke, hold your thumb over the neck, and give it a good shake. It is a very delicate operation requiring perfect timing. The idea is to insert the tip of the bottle into the vagina just as you move your thumb, so that the contents will explode *in* you, not *on* you.

I used up a whole six-pack. I finally got the last one in, more or less, but by that time I was covered with Coke. I had also screamed, "Oh, shit!" which is a word that Southern men think ladies don't know. When I stood up at last, my thighs stuck together.

By this time it was almost dawn, and I had to hurry back to the dorm before it grew light. My beau suggested that we could save time if we cut through the churchyard, but a warning signal went off in my brain. The night had already been marked by that *je ne sais quoi* that I tend to bring to things, like the time I almost got run over by the Bloodmobile. I am a female Dagwood. I *knew* that if we cut through the churchyard I would fall into an open grave, so we took the long way home.

I didn't get P.G. that night, either. In fact, I never have.

4

"WALTZ ME AROUND AGAIN, WILLIE"
or The Forty-Niner

A man need not be middle-aged to be a Forty-Niner, though it helps. Basically it is a state of mind marked by bumptiousness. Only a Forty-Niner could say to a woman, as one said to me: "I guarantee you the best time in bed you've ever had, Scout's honor."

His chief problem is an inferiority complex, a fact noted by Hans Habe in *The Wounded Land*: "Sooner or later European men experience the envious hostility of American men." The Forty-Niner's fear that he is not romantic (French-Latin), strong (Teutonic), or polished (British) is what makes him behave as he does.

Our Forty-Niner is named William "Bill" Fletcher. This is the way his business cards are printed, and this is how he spelled his name on his posters when he ran for city council back home. It is also written this way on the personalized matchbooks and ball-point pens that he had made up back home, which he hands out as icebreakers and conversation pieces to anyone who sits next to him in a public place.

William "Bill" Fletcher is from Back Home, U.S.A., but the best place to find him is in Out of Town, U.S.A., where he spends a lot of time conventioneering, paging and being paged, and saying "Hit me again" to bartenders. On these occasions he wears a name tag that reads William "Bill" Fletcher, but he himself has *husband* written all over him. Forty-Niners seem to have been born married. When I was in France I saw countless middle-aged businessmen, but none had his *look*. I kept wondering, "Where are all the married men?" until I realized finally that the look to which I was accustomed is uniquely American. As Sinclair Lewis said of Babbitt: "He seemed prosperous, extremely married, and unromantic."

William "Bill" Fletcher is so outgoing and other-directed that he has peer groups instead of genes. Being with him is like being stuck in a hotel room with nothing to read but *The Toastmaster's Handbook*. His tone is one of determined affability without surcease. His conversation is onerous due to his firm belief that women cannot talk intelligently. He, therefore, must carry the ball. He is the sort that Jack Nichols wrote about in *Men's Liberation*, who believes that when talking to a woman, a man's conversation must be "carefully mapped, full of interesting tidbits, masterful, forceful, alluring, and knowledgeable, all at the same time." Thanks to his conviction that a woman will not respect him unless he deals in facts, his conversation usually sounds as if it ought to be preceded by a bosun's pipe and a voice bellowing *Now Hear This!*

He is a devotee of Twenty Questions. "What do you want out of life?" he asks soulfully, his eyes narrowing into pensive slits. He has a perfect genius for putting this question to a woman who already has what she wants. Inevitably, she reacts with irritation, which makes him smile knowingly and ask his next question: "What are you so unhappy about?" When she replies that she is perfectly happy, thank you, he shakes his head, smiles his worldly-wise smile and says: "Tell me what you're afraid of."

It goes on like this, complete with "What do you do for fun?"

and "Don't you ever get lonely?" until things begin to sound like country music song titles, especially if the lady is lured into answers like: "I went jogging in the rain yesterday morning." He wants desperately to prove that all career women are melancholy, sex-starved waifs, so any woman being grilled by him finds herself trying very hard to sound busy, sophisticated, and well-rounded. One of his standard verbal traps is his comparison between life in New York and life in Back Home. Under no condition should a woman say: "I hate small towns because they're so dull," because William "Bill" Fletcher will come back with: "You like excitement, huh? Hee-hee-hee," accompanied by all the appropriate gleams and winks. His conversational terrain is full of such land mines, so always say that you love small towns.

William "Bill" Fletcher is always thinking ahead to his next question while the lady is still answering the last one, which makes her so tense that soon she is thinking ahead to her next answer while he is still posing the next question. Soon nobody is listening to anybody, and nothing makes sense. He calls this sort of thing "getting her to open up."

After Twenty Questions comes Q.E.D. time. His favorite entry is, of course, "Football builds character." Argue with him and he will simply say: "But it builds character." Continue arguing with him and you will be told: "Women don't understand what football means to guys." Ask what football means to guys and he will reply: "It builds character."

Almost as dear to his heart is that other self-evident proposition: "Only a man can play the violin because it's like getting a response out of a woman's body." This one is perilously close to the comment made by Balzac that an inept lover is like an orangutan with a violin. Somewhere, somehow, William "Bill" Fletcher has heard this quotation. He has also seen *Murders in the Rue Morgue,* so it is never long before he recites: "Edgar Allan Poe said never give a monkey a violin."

Do not try to untangle this because he will only punch you in the ribs and boom: "Hey, the party's getting serious! What're we going to do, sit here and talk about lit'rechoor?" Worse, any mention of Balzac has an excellent chance of turning into a joke about Zach's balls. Under no condition should you encourage William "Bill" Fletcher's scintillating wit because he will then turn to the waiter and order a tray of "whore's drawers" to go with your cocktails. Other favorites in this category are the definition of a French breakfast, "a roll in bed with honey"; the virility of the author of *She*, "ride 'er haggard"; the surname of the author of *The Odyssey*, "Homer Who?"; and the outcome of *The Rape of the Lock*, "Here comes the key!" If you do not shriek with laughter over these offerings, William "Bill" Fletcher will put a comforting arm around your shoulders and inform you, as he informed me, that you would really be a great gal if only you would develop a sense of humor.

When he is with a woman he finds desirable, he likes to talk about physical matters. He would prefer to talk about actual sex, but he is not sure how she would react; so he tests her by steering the conversation around to other bodily functions. Two extremely popular topics are vomiting and diarrhea. His favorite saga is the time he had tourist tummy in Mexico. Any woman with an Elizabethan streak is advised to stifle her amusement because if she laughs, William "Bill" Fletcher will take it as a sign that he can talk about *real* sex.

If he is a war veteran, and he nearly always is, his subject matter becomes fecal matter even more quickly. Any mere civilian can have diarrhea, but only men who fight for their country can boast of dysentery. This ailment is much sexier conversational fare to his way of thinking because it is a kind of war wound, and hence more masculine. He describes his Guadalcanal stomach cramps—"the grips, Jesus"—and gives his lady listener a trot-by-trot account of how he ran, bent double, to the latrine. The word *latrine* turns him on no end because it, too, is exclusively masculine. Women have dozens of euphemisms for *toilet* but *latrine* has never been one of them.

Thanks to William "Bill" Fletcher, I know how to dig a latrine and how to construct a bamboo enclosure. It is a shame I am too old to be drafted for combat duty in the brave new world that ERA supporters are currently holding out to women because my country needs me. I could be Saint Joan of the Shovel. I owe it all to William "Bill" Fletcher, who drew a diagram of a latrine under construction for me on a soggy cocktail napkin one night in the King Cole lounge of the St. Regis.

Drawing pictures and maps to illustrate his remarks is a sure sign of a Forty-Niner. "This is Guadalcanal, and this here's the lagoon. Here's the beach where we landed, and over here is where I found the Jap colonel in the cave with the chickens." He goes on to say that the Jap colonel was "taking a crap" when he looked up and into the barrel of William "Bill" Fletcher's rifle. This is how Daddy won the war. I know, I have the soggy napkins to prove it.

The third or fourth drink brings him to the scabby-whore confession. Usually an Oriental, this is a woman that only a James Jones hero could love—sort of earthy around the edges from holding court in a ditch. It is not necessary to offer her a whole pack of cigarettes because she will do it for one, or even for a butt. She always has missing teeth or is completely toothless, and she has scabs on her legs.

The average woman will ask, "But how *could* you sleep with a woman like that?" This is exactly what William "Bill" Fletcher wants her to ask. He smiles—sadly, sheepishly, and proudly, all at the same time—and replies: "When a guy is really horny, he'll take anything that walks on two legs." Hardly a compliment to the lady he is trying to seduce, but then it was not meant to be. He is complimenting himself by saying, in effect, that he is *that* highly sexed. The message he is sending across the table is: "If I were potent with a wreck like her, think what I'll be like with *you*."

It never occurs to him that his lady friend places a different interpretation upon his scabby-whore confession. If, by some strange twist of hormones, a woman were horny enough to sleep with a toothless, scabby man, she would *never* admit it. Her pride would keep her lips sealed forever because women hate above all to be pitied in sexual situations. To the female mind, anyone who would settle for a partner like that is a loser.

William "Bill" Fletcher believes that he must sprinkle his conversation with jokes that appear to spring naturally from the subject matter—which means that when he senses it is time for a joke, he speeds up what he is saying, finishes it quickly, and then says: "That reminds me of a story." He is especially fond of the true anecdote with a joke-like punch line because it has more immediacy and makes him look to a woman's eyes like a man who is always There when important people do and say important things.

William "Bill" Fletcher told me the following story one night at dinner:

Willie Mays was the first black to join an all-white country club. One day in the locker room, a white man who did not recognize him said, "Hey, boy, bring me a towel." Mays played along and brought him the towel.

I did not think the story was hilarious, so I simply smiled wryly. My mistake was not bursting into gales of laughter along with William "Bill" Fletcher because he does not like wry smiles, especially from women. *Any* lack of response from a woman is to him a lack of sexual response. By smiling instead of laughing aloud I had, in effect, experienced mild pleasure but not orgasm. So William "Bill" Fletcher kept on pumping away. He took a forkful of mashed potato, then said, "Hey, boy, bring me a towel, ha-ha." When I smiled again—more tightly this time—he took a swallow of water and said, "Hey, boy, bring me a towel. Mays really showed him, didn't he?" This time the corner of my mouth merely twitched, so William "Bill" Fletcher ate a piece of steak and said, "Hey, boy, bring me a towel! Mays couldn't have handled it any better, could he?"

The Forty-Niner who repeats his punch line, often with an accompanying elbow to a woman's ribs, is symbolically ramming away at her cervix in a desperate attempt to send her over the top. Female self-containment frightens him. He is terrified of formality in a woman. Saying "How do you do" instead of "Hi," or calling him "Mr. Fletcher" will wound him to the quick. He also requires lots of smiles; if he does not see them he will chide: "Why so serious? It can't be that bad!" A pensive woman is a sexually unresponsive woman to him, and he must cheer her up or else his shaky self-esteem will collapse. The epidemic of smiles that attacks the traveler the moment he sets foot in an airline terminal is intended for the Forty-Niner. Ticket agents, stewardesses, Hertz girls, and that *risus sardonicus* known as an Official Greeter are all hired primarily to have "orgasms" in public.

By the same token, any *no* from a woman is a sexual no. If he asks his secretary to work overtime and she says, "I'm sorry, I can't," he feels subconsciously that she has refused him sex— his crestfallen look gives him away every time. If he offers a woman on a plane his little plastic pyramid of cashews and she says no, thank you, it has the same effect on him. Refusal from a woman, no matter how minor, sets up a panic in him that leads him into that maddening Forty-Niner habit of *cajoling*. Does she want his copy of *Business Week*? No. Would she like to change seats with him so that she can sit by the window and see the New York skyline? No. Because he is a product of the era that claimed a woman always means the opposite of what she says, he will press on, burrowing through her refusals like a mole. He must get a yes out of her, no matter how meaningless a yes it is.

He also needs to be seen getting a response out of her. Many Forty-Niners travel together to conventions, but they do not always manage to sit together. If one of the group is seated next to a woman, his cronies keep a close eye on how he is doing and wink at him as they go back and forth to the john. If his female seatmate does not take his magazine or his pyramid of cashews, *if she will not talk to him*, he is certain to hear about it later.

When I was returning home after a publicity tour—not the best time to get a response out of a writer—William "Bill" Fletcher urged on me his magazine, his copy of *Jaws*, a pillow, a Sight Saver to wipe my reading glasses, and finally his nuts.

The fact that I was drinking bourbon steadily made him even more persistent, because the Forty-Niner always thinks that a woman who drinks is more available than one who does not— thanks to "his peasant-like delight in petty vices," as H. L. Mencken put it.* When we disembarked, he had offered me everything but his vomit bag and been turned down each time, to the rather sadistic delight of his cronies, who rode him with loud taunts of "Hey, you really struck out with that one."

The woman who automatically says "No, thank you" instead of merely "No" in such situations is in for it because the Forty-Niner will grasp at any straw. He takes simple good manners as encouragement; if a woman is too polite, he thinks he is already in. "No, thank you" being two more words than necessary to get her meaning across, the Forty-Niner believes himself to be in a conversation with her. Thus he forces her to become increasingly curt, until she is biting off her "no's" like cashews. A woman often has no choice but to be rude to William "Bill" Fletcher, but even then she cannot get rid of him because he is a product of the *Gone With the Wind* school of sexual interpretation. He firmly believes that the worse a woman treats him, the better she really likes him—only like Scarlett, she doesn't know it.

* In Defense of Women.

It was the Forty-Niner who puzzled Alexis de Tocqueville 150 years ago during his tour of America:

> I have often noticed in the United States that it is not easy to make a man understand that his presence may be dispensed with; hints will not always suffice to shake him off. I contradict an American at every word he says, to show him that his conversation bores me; he instantly labors with fresh pertinacity to convince me; I preserve a dogged silence, and he thinks I am meditating deeply on the truths that he is uttering; at last I rush from his company, and he supposes that some urgent business hurries me elsewhere. This man will never understand that he wearies me to death unless I tell him so, and the only way to get rid of him is to make him my enemy for life.*

When *I* want to get rid of him I use the non sequitur technique. I guarantee its success provided you can keep a straight face. I can. Anyone who has seen me on television knows that I have but one facial expression: Anglo-Saxon indigestion.

When a Forty-Niner on the prowl asks his usual, "Can I buy you a drink?" reply:

"The annexation of Schleswig-Holstein drove King Christian mad."

"Huh? Hey, would you run that by me again?"

"The Empress Eudoxia, mother of Theodosius II, exiled Saint John Chrysostom from Constantinople."

"Hey, come on, what is this?"

"Hypatia was murdered by Peter the Reader, who cut her throat with oyster shells in the year 416 A.D."

Remember to stay well within the bounds of trivia. Do not

---

* Democracy in America, Vol. II.

say, for example: "The Duke of Clarence was shooting in Scotland in August of 1888, so he could not have been Jack the Ripper." All Forty-Niners have heard about Jack the Ripper so any mention of him will get you into a conversation. Schleswig-Holstein is ideal, and so is Bosnia-Herzegovina. If you can last long enough, William "Bill" Fletcher will shuffle off, shaking his head and muttering, "Jeez, that broad is crazy."

To women my age who started work in the fifties, the Forty-Niner is the Boss, destined to be linked forever in our minds with dead-end secretarial jobs. He is our deus ex machina: the throat-clearing, coughing, hacking, spitting, rambling, ungrammatical sciolist on the Dictaphone. Any woman who has typed his letters has brushed close to madness.

Thanks to the Forty-Niner, secretaries of the fifties were linguistic curmudgeons long before Edwin Newman won the crown. Much of the language usage to which Newman objects is traceable to sexually insecure men trying desperately to impress women.

The Forty-Niner's appalling ignorance makes him seem more uncouth than he actually is. His ignorance is not his fault. He is a lifelong victim of forced specialization. Many Forty-Niners are my slide-rule beaux of twenty-two years ago. The thigh is plumper now but the leather Excalibur is still going slap-slap against it. They are also the boys who majored in business administration because it seemed the masculine thing to do. Forty-Niners were influenced by Depression-traumatized fathers who warned them incessantly against the perils of becoming a jack-of-all-trades, and urged them to "find one thing you can do, and then do it."

While the boys were settling themselves into the narrow end of the funnel, we girls branched out. Since everybody knew that no girl could get a good job anyway, nobody cared if we took Latin or medieval literature. What the era called a "broad general education" would enable us to circulate at our husbands' business gatherings trailing bons mots along with Arpège. My education enabled me to stay sane. An evening with Cicero or Racine helped me recover from a day with a Forty-Niner boss. It is exquisitely satisfying to read "How long will you abuse our patience, Cataline?" after a day spent typing "This is the house by the side of the road with the white fence and the green shingles that need painting that Fletcher Realty built."

Thanks to fifties sexism, women turned into interesting people while men turned into idiots savants. The Forty-Niner knows all there is to know about copper fittings or actuarial tables but nothing about anything else. Despite his breezy exterior, he is not happy with the situation. His intellectual frustration makes him subject to abrupt and often bizarre epistemological cravings.

One night William "Bill" Fletcher and I were eating spaghetti in an Italian restaurant when suddenly, apropos of nothing, he looked up and said: "You know, talking about lichee nuts . . ."

I looked up with a start.

"You know," he went on, "they say that if you crack open a lichee nut, inside there's another lichee nut. And inside that one there's another one. And on and on and on. Did you ever think of that?"

"You're defining infinity," I said.

"Nah! Hey, the party's getting serious! Come on, don't go getting deep on me."

"It *is* infinity that you're talking about."

"Nah! No, no, no, listen, let me explain it to you. See, if you took a picture of me, right? Then you took another picture of me holding the first picture, right? Inside the second picture would be a picture of me holding a picture of me, and on and on and on. It would never end, right? Think of that."

His dismissive *Nah!* is his warning to himself not to let the conversation get too intellectual, yet an intellectual conversation is precisely what he craves. He longs to talk but he does not dare because ruminative intellectualizing is not acceptable in Back Home, U.S.A. Nobody in these friendly hamlets listens, really listens, to anybody else, and the worst offender is Mrs. Fletcher herself.

Now in her early forties, Betty Fletcher is the same simple, outgoing girl she was in college—the one who filled the dorm with the ululating shriek of her favorite record, "Love Is a Many-Splendored Thing" played by the Fifty Thousand Violins. It was the homing pitch on the dog whistle of her ambition. She was dying to get married then, and she is dying to stay married now. She is terrified by the thought of divorce. This is a woman who would rather be married than conscious.

When William "Bill" Fletcher says his wife does not understand him, he is telling the truth. She does not want to understand him because she is afraid of what she might discover if she did. She thinks constantly about other women and is ever on the lookout for signs that William "Bill" Fletcher has developed a roving eye. If he exhibits the smallest evidence of discontent, all sorts of warning bells go off in her brain. To Betty, a ruminative conversation is a sign of discontent; so William "Bill" Fletcher has learned not to initiate them. They would only go like this:

"You know, talking about lichee nuts. . . . They say that if you crack open a lichee nut, inside there's another one. And inside that there's another one. And on and on and on. It would never stop, until the last bird had carried the last grain of sand from the last mountain across the last drop of water in the last ocean. Did you ever think of that?"

"What's the matter?"

"Nothing. I was just thinking about how things go on and on."

"Are you worried about something?"

"No! I'm just thinking about what's *out* there. I just got to thinking about that old Chinese story about the lichee nuts. Those Chinese can really make you start thinking about things."

"I could have made sweet and sour pork out of those spareribs, but I thought you felt like sauerkraut."

God forbid that he should try discussing that other favorite, déjà vu. The moment he said, "You know that feeling that you've been somewhere before or met somebody before?" poor Betty's divorce-programed brain would start spinning like a cartwheel with visions of women on planes, women at parties, newly hired schoolteachers, old motels under new management, and the latest crop of IBM wives.

Women like Betty are always their own worst enemies. After a few acrostic conversations with her, William "Bill" Fletcher will fall like a ripe plum into the lap of any woman who will talk to him. Once, while having a drink with him, I remembered a point of grammar that one of Mary McCarthy's characters cherished, so more out of desperation than anything else, I said: "You know, we say *Aren't I?* which is a contraction of *Are I not*, which we never say. Shouldn't we really say *Amn't I?*"

His eyes lit with that unique sparkle that is intellectual curiosity.

"Hey! Hey, you're right! I never thought about that before, but by damn, it's true. Amn't I! By God, I'm going to say that from now on. Hey, Charlie, amn't I smart?"

It touched me more than any of the extravagant compliments he had been paying me. I could have cried.

William "Bill" Fletcher lives in a sexual time capsule labeled "1940." Subconsciously, he still believes what he heard behind the barn:

1. Divorced women are easy because they've been there, they

know the score. Once a woman gets used to getting it regular, she can't do without it.

2. Nurses are easy because they fool around with naked bodies, which makes them stay hot all the time. Nurses are also clean, you can't get the clap from them because they know how to take care of themselves. They can get their hands on the right medicine.

3. Only nice girls have illegitimate kids. If a bad girl gets knocked up, she knows where to get her hands on the right medicine.

4. If a girl goes down on you, that means she goes down on everybody, so never kiss her on the mouth.

It may seem incredible that any man in the seventies is still thinking about ergot and mercury, but psychologically, William "Bill" Fletcher has inherited a pro kit. Ergot and mercury are to him what Antietam and Manassas are to many Southerners. He simply will not forget about them.

Sexual class-consciousness is another ingredient of his time capsule. It was not really so very long ago that the "shop girl" was the primary extracurricular outlet for men on the prowl, along with the waitress and the blue-collar woman. After them came the "office wife" of the thirties and forties, who can still be found in the hinterlands where he is from. She is available to her boss and perhaps to visiting firemen, and she tends to be rather pathetic and resigned to it all.

When William "Bill" Fletcher blows into New York and goes skirt chasing, it is this kind of woman he subconsciously seeks. He does not find her. Big-city girls now have professional-level jobs, and even those who are still secretaries are extremely soignée. Judy O'Grady is now indistinguishable from the colonel's lady, and a surprising number of Forty-Niners have no idea how to cope with her. How can they buy the poor kid a good meal if she looks like the girl in the "Charlie" ads?

In *Lonely in America*, Suzanne Gordon quotes a habituée of a singles bar on what usually happens when William "Bill" Fletcher tangles with big-city girls.

A guy from Texas, in his forties, who comes to New York on a convention, he's staying at the Americana, he's married, and he comes up here and thinks he's going to knock the world dead. He'll offer the girl the world, and she won't fuck in the end; at least if she got the guy off in the end, then he'd get what he wanted, the guy thinks he's going to come to New York and it's going to be easy, but it's not that easy, because these girls look at these guys as the jerks of the world, as real saps.

I occasionally run into Forty-Niner class-consciousness. I am a night person. I write all night and stop at dawn, then take a walk as soon as it gets light. The joggers are always out in full force but I am obviously not one of them. I wear regular clothes and always carry my handbag even though I'm not planning to shop because I would feel naked without it. On numerous occasions, Forty-Niners have stopped their cars and tried to pick me up. This never happens at other times of the day. I finally realized what was causing it. They think I am on my way to work, and any woman who goes to work at such an hour must be either a waitress or a factory hand—available, in other words.

Casanova wrote that for men, "love is three-quarters curiosity." In *The Need to Be Loved*, Theodore Reik observed: "Nothing in the psychology of women can be compared to the sexual inquisitiveness of the male."

William "Bill" Fletcher is America's foremost sexual quidnunc. If you work for him, he will quiz you relentlessly on your

sex life, usually couching his queries in avuncular language,
like: "How's the boyfriend situation?" If you answer his first
question, he gets his toe in the door. Once that happens he will
press you with: "Going out tonight? . . . Big weekend? . . . Going
to Bermuda? Bet you come back without a suntan, hee-hee-
hee."

His best sexual experiences occur in his mind, which is why
he spends so much time sitting and staring at women with his
eyes squinched up and his mouth tilted in one of those kouroi
smiles found on Archaic Greek statues. Every woman is familiar with his speculative gaze across a restaurant or lobby. It is
one of the few times that he is quiet and still. He stares and
stares, like a teenage boy standing in the street gazing at the
home of a teacher on whom he has a crush. He prefers to
believe that his curiosity is exclusively sexual, but it is not.
Twenty years with Betty have done their work. He married her
because she was safe, predictable, and unthreatening, and now
he has begun to reap the harvest of his youthful caution. He
knows *nothing* about women, and so he has developed an
insatiable need to know *everything* about us. His longing to *know*
transcends mere physical details; he is a man in search of she-
ness.

He wants to probe a woman's mind as well as her body, but
he does not dare. If he asked her what she thinks, she might tell
him, and thereby render him into A Man Who Understands
Women—i.e., a man with a dangerously large, even homosex-
ually large feminine component in his makeup. The fun would
be over then; he could no longer go out with the boys and talk
about how hard it is to understand women. Worse, the boys
might start having trouble understanding *him.* . . . So goes his
reasoning, and it always leads him to the same old dead end.
He is like Babbitt, who tried to save his sanity by changing his
ways, only to find the forces of Zenith arrayed against him. He
has no choice but to do what Babbitt did and revert to type, so

he puts the lid on his deeper speculations about women and concentrates on that favorite Forty-Niner question: "I wonder what she's like in the sack?"

He knows all the "signs" of a hot tomato when he sees one; they come out of his sexual time capsule, too. A woman who wears a red dress is asking for it. A woman who kicks her foot back and forth is signaling him. A woman who slips off her shoes is hot—not just her feet, but all of her. A woman whose eyes slant down toward the bridge of her nose is hot. A woman who smokes a lot likes to go down on men. A woman waiting on the corner is a prostitute. A woman having a drink alone doesn't really want the drink, she wants a man. *All* unescorted women want to be picked up. There are women, women everywhere, lurking in wait for him, signaling him, kicking their bare feet back and forth like babies in a high chair, smoking their lungs out as they drool over mental pictures of the Fletcher penis.

Fate has set me up for William "Bill" Fletcher because my eyes slant, my feet are flat, and I was born with no sense of direction whatsoever. I constantly get lost in New York, which involves a lot of standing in utter perplexity on corners wondering where I am. Because I take so many wrong turns, I end up walking an extra mile or so, which makes my archless feet hurt. When I finally limp back to my hotel, I am parched, so I go to the cocktail lounge, order a drink, light a cigarette, and take off my shoes.

> *Though by the wayside she fell,*
> *She may yet mend her ways;*
> *Some poor old mother is waiting for her*
> *Who has seen better days.*

William "Bill" Fletcher's standard line is "God, you're lovely." A conservative to his bone marrow, he cannot recognize quaintness and he distrusts change on principle. To borrow his idiom, once he has run something up the flagpole and seen it wave, he will not relinquish it. If "God, you're lovely" worked once, it will work for all time. In the realm of seduction, his motto is: "The law of the Medes and the Persians altereth not."

When he thinks he scents sure nooky, he will assure a woman that she is safe with him because he "wouldn't hurt a fly." This one goes back to 82 A.D. and the reign of the Roman Emperor Domitian, who liked to catch flies and impale them on pins so he could watch them suffer. One day a senator asked the palace chamberlain if anyone was with the emperor and the chamberlain replied: "No, not even a fly."

Most Forty-Niners have one supreme seduction technique that they "swear by," as they tell their cronies. Because they believe that all women are equally gullible, they will use their favorite ploy indiscriminately, without regard for the possible perspicacity of any one individual woman. The hero of *Some Came Running*, Dave Hirsh, set out to seduce the most intelligent woman he had ever met with an original poem that he had used successfully on seven other women.

> The more powerful and dramatic method was to seem to write the poem right in front of them; get thoughtful, ask for paper and pencil, and—with proper hesitations every now and then for thinking—pretend to create the poem right there.... He had used this method four of the seven times, and it always created a very powerful and emotional effect. ... The other way was—usually after some evening of particularly heavy lovemaking which ended in frustration—to show up with the poem next day and say he'd written it that night when he got home, had sat up all night writing it.

Dave "writes" his love poem to Gwen French, but she is not nearly so gullible as the other girls. She spoils the effect by laughing in his face.

The Forty-Niner is always predictable in his approach to love. In John Marquand's novel, *B. F.'s Daughter*, Polly Fulton knew exactly what her Air Force colonel was going to do and say from the moment she met him at a party, and as things turned out, she was right.

> There was the usual tiresome business of saying that she could go downtown perfectly well by herself, and the colonel saying that she certainly could not. And there was the tiresome business of not being too emphatic about it. She was not sure how Colonel Beyers would behave alone in the taxi, but he behaved very well, considering. He was suddenly so considerate and silent that Polly found herself saying those things that everyone always said, such as, "I've had an awfully nice time," which encouraged him to put his arm around her.

Polly finds that the colonel's total resemblance to every other man of his ilk she has met in wartime New York is so strong that she is numbed. She does not want to invite him upstairs but she does it anyway. Woodenly, she offers him a drink, and he accompanies her to the kitchen.

> ... saying, as of course he would, that he was wonderful in a kitchen. Then there was that usual business of holding the ice cubes under the hot water tap and of having them fall into the sink and washing them.

When they return to the living room, the colonel recites his line—"You're a lovely, lonely enigmatic character" and then makes a pass, which brings Polly out of her trance at last. "Suddenly the whole thing became a sordid, vulgar, meaningless surrender and she wrenched herself away."

Women are always emerging from trances and wrenching

away from a Forty-Niner, which is why he is always exclaiming, "What did I do? What did I say?"

It has been said that a woman is so easily distracted during sex that a ringing phone or a flapping blind can ruin her fun. William "Bill" Fletcher can manage much worse distractions than that. In fact, he could make a fortune in the movies as a special effects man.

Following a woman into the kitchen is a standard Forty-Niner maneuver that you can count on. Like Polly's colonel, William "Bill" Fletcher followed me into my kitchen when I went to open a bottle of wine. I had trouble with the cork, so in his masterful way, he took the bottle from me and put it between his knees.

"There's a trick to this," he said confidently, looking up at me with a wink.

Suddenly, the cork crumbled, the corkscrew gave way, and he hit himself in the crotch. As he lay moaning on my bed, I remembered that I did not own an icebag so I improvised one from one of his condoms.

William "Bill" Fletcher is as suspicious of "serious" girls as he was in college. Serious is his code word for intelligent. For his Out of Town sprees, he prefers what he calls "a girl who likes to have a good time." This is the girl who nicknames herself Buffie during adolescence and refuses to answer to anything else. Buffie is a female version of William "Bill" Fletcher: she makes a lot of noise, embarrasses herself and others, and always has a whale of a good time on those exhausting evenings when everybody runs from nightclub to nightclub in that activity known as "doing the town."

Buffie and William "Bill" Fletcher would rather do towns than each other. Both are typical American puritans who deliberately wear themselves out in late-night carouses so that they will be too tired to do anything in bed that might create a threatening sexual situation. When they finally do get into bed,

Buffie closes her bleary eyes, opens her legs, and pats the back of William "Bill" Fletcher's neck while he labors over her. He talks a lot about hot women, but all he really wants is cooperation, the exhausted woman's specialty.

A "serious" girl would never want to hit twelve nightclubs. She would not find it hilarious when a haggard chanteuse sings "The Swelling of the Organ and the Coming of the Bride." This is William "Bill" Fletcher's idea of risqué, but the "serious" girl knows better. She would not be overjoyed to run into one of William "Bill" Fletcher's friends ("Hey, look, it's Charlie! Hey, Charlie! C'mon over!") and she has no wish to sing "Deep in the Heart of Texas" at three in the morning. She simply wants to go to bed, which makes her a threat to William "Bill" Fletcher. His sex must be preceded by a fireman's ball so that afterward he can tell himself: "Aw, we just went out and had a good time." It is less adulterous this way.

Meanwhile, back in Back Home, Betty is doing what she has been doing for the last twenty years: cutting out articles on How to Make Your Marriage Work. She might as well put down her scissors because William "Bill" Fletcher will never leave her. In fact, he worries that she will leave *him*. He is a firm believer in the traditionalist view of the sexes that George Gilder promulgated in *Sexual Suicide*. According to this view, women must socialize men in the name of civilization, else the world will sink back into primeval ooze. Men without women become menaces, to themselves as well as to others; the wilderness beckons every man who is not saved by the love of a good woman.

If Betty ever left William "Bill" Fletcher, he would react like Frank Hirsh in *Some Came Running*, who comes home to find Agnes gone.

> ... sitting in the clothes-strewn living room, the note dangling from his hand, he began to cry ... the nameless, frightened, lonely panic: at the thought of living here all

alone the rest of his life: at the thought of having to clean this house up himself: at the thought of having to keep it clean: at the thought of eating meals in restaurants greasy spoons, all the rest of his life or of ineffectually trying to cook them himself: at the thought of the laundry room and of trying to run the mangle: how could he ever do that? who would he get to do that for him: but most of all at the thought of walking echoingly back and forth through this house, alone, all the rest of his life. No Agnes.

To calm himself, Frank has a drink, but his hands are shaking so badly he spills the whiskey.

Capless, the bottle had fallen over and most of its remaining contents had run out on the rug. Staring at it, the deep, un-nameable, unbearable panic seized him again. Frantically, he ran out to the kitchen and got the dishrag and wet it and grabbed some dishtowels and ran back in to try and clean it up.... It was a very poor effort at cleaning, and it did not even assuage his conscience: Here he was, ruining their house, his and Agnes's house, almost before she had even left it. Guilt of a power and strength unknown to him before gripped him as he tried to clean it up.... My God! what would he do if she didn't come back? The whole place would sink into rack and ruin and decay; and he himself would de-scend into sloth and dirt and stagnation. A bum. She just had to come back! She just had to!

William "Bill" Fletcher's tendency to run in packs of other Forty-Niners usually results in ludicrous situations, but some-times they exude a deadly quality that can make a woman feel like a doe in the forest during hunting season. Once, while I was having dinner alone in New York, a gang of Forty-Niners burst through the door intent upon "having a good time."

Nothing happened, but the possibility of a scene ruined my

evening and my dinner. I felt a tension growing in me, a waiting, a conviction that someone would say something nasty, or that there would be a crash ... that *something was going to happen*. My tension mounted until I was as jumpy as a paranoid flea. If someone had brushed me with a finger I would have gone through the roof.

Suddenly a thought crossed my mind: "This must be the way Jews feel." As I pursued this speculation, I understood, for the first time, the underlying meaning of the Yiddish word *goyish*. It means more than "gentile"; it means William "Bill" Fletcher with all his stops pulled out. It means men with too much to drink talking in voices that are too loud, picking fights, grabbing waitresses, practicing football plays in lobbies, and in general indulging in that fine old *shaygets* tradition known as "horsing around."

Most of all, *goyish* means men traveling together. William "Bill" Fletcher is a gentile phenomenon; Jewish men simply do not carouse, probably because carousing starts with heavy drinking and Jews are not heavy drinkers. One sees perhaps two or three Jewish men dining together for a business-related reason, but more than two or three Jews equals an Israeli Bond banquet, and then there are two or three hundred, with wives. Seven or eight or a dozen Jewish men roaring around alone is simply un-Jewish.

Jews and women both have good reason to fear a group of men on a spree. I suspect that the real reason behind the mutual attraction of Jewish men and gentile women has little to do with the tiresome business about retroussé noses or that old saw, "They make such good husbands." They are drawn to each other by the subconscious knowledge that they have a common potential enemy in the Fletcher-pack.

In conclusion, as they say in *The Toastmaster's Handbook*, William "Bill" Fletcher would not be so bad as a sex partner if only one could put a bag over his personality. It is my fervent wish that he would study the advice of Lord Chesterfield:

Talk often, but never long; in that case, if you do not please, at least you are sure not to tire your hearers.

Tell stories very seldom, and absolutely never but where they are very apt and very short. Omit every circumstance that is not material, and beware of digressions. To have frequent recourse to narrative betrays great want of imagination.

One man affirms that he has ridden post a hundred miles in six hours. Probably it is a lie, but supposing it to be true, what then? Why, he is a very good post boy, that is all.

Loud laughter is the mirth of the mob.

Never hold anybody by the button or the hand in order to be heard out; for if people are not willing to hear you, you had much better hold your tongue than them.

5

SWEET SAVAGE
SUPPORTIVENESS
or The Liberated Man

The historical novel is back, more popular than ever thanks to the advent of Jonathan Stuart Mill, the Liberated Man. After coping with Jonathan, a woman is bound to become a historical novel junkie because he is so plagued by options and viable alternatives that he cannot get his swash to buckle when she needs her buckle swashed.

Jonathan is so liberated that he has lost the knack of being a man, so it is never long before his girl friend takes over. She starts to become eerily like John Wayne. When they go together to the lumberyard to pick out new bookshelves, she points without hesitation to the wood she wants and says, "Okay, Jonathan, let's move it out!"

Blacks are very well acquainted with Jonathan. During the Civil Rights movement he drove *them* crazy. Now, though, he has forgotten all about the "Nee-gro" except to send the NAACP five dollars a year. His famous conscience is not troubled by this ungenerous sum because he has found a new cause: feminism. He is now "into women," as he says with a straight face.

Actually he is not because the vagina is "out" now. The clitoris is the latest thing, so ever-trendy Jonathan has become a clitoromaniac. His odes to this organ sound like Burns' "wee sleekit beastie" tribute to the mouse. The clitoris is the whistle-stop between maidenhead and personhood on Jonathan's train of thought, and he will not bypass it. He rubs it, he tickles it, he licks it for hours until his girl friend becomes inflamed, though not the way Jonathan planned. She ends up in the gynecologist's office with a case of Jonathanorrhea.

Jonathan was not always so eager to please women. In college he talked a lot about "chicks" and was often heard to say: "If you don't go on the Pill, you'll never see me again." Like the protagonist of Gail Parent's novel, *David Meyer Is a Mother*, Jonathan used to pride himself on being able to unhook a bra with two fingers, but now that so many women no longer wear them, the realization that his former masculine techniques are now old-fashioned fills him with panic. More than anything else, Jonathan fears being tagged as a reactionary. Now that *masculine* and *reactionary* are practically synonymous, he tumbles into an abyss of guilt and self-hatred and becomes an andro-phobe.

Like all guilt-ridden people, Jonathan likes to make public confessions of past sins. He can make a cocktail party sound like an AA meeting: "My name is Jonathan Stuart Mill and I used to be a male chauvinist pig." He lists all the ways in which he used to be "insensitive to women's problems" and then describes how it was the day he saw the light—a kind of Bernadette-at-the-grotto experience notable for the many clichés it inspires, such as: "I stood there . . . suddenly I realized . . . I became two people, half of me was standing off to the side looking at the other half." Finally he utters the supreme cliché that makes him sound like the Gothic heroine that he is: "If I had only known!"

Nowadays, any man who does much reading is certain to feel

like the wormwood star in the Book of Revelations. Articles on rape, wife-beating, child molestation, and other male sins are everywhere. Jonathan reads all the time, so he has become the foremost victim of our current antimale national mood. The standard lead on the kind of articles Jonathan reads is: "Men commit over ninety percent of all violent crimes."

When Jonathan is not reading he watches "relevant" television shows, i.e., the kind on which gimlet-eyed radical feminists discuss the finer points of setting fire to sleeping husbands. Nora Efron wrote in her *TV Guide* column that "television is preoccupied by the subject of male brutes," and expressed shock over the Phil Donahue interview with the battered wife who revenged herself with a connubial *Götterdämmerung.* Commented Miss Efron: "She roasted the man alive. And as she described this act, the audience of middle-class Philadelphia ladies gave her an explosive hand of applause."

Jonathan, who is also preoccupied by the subject of male brutes, gets the message—it is burn, baby, burn. Masochistically he reflects on it. Gradually he becomes aware of a little glimmer of hostility flickering within him. Horror of horrors, he realizes that he *hates* women who set fire to men. The hatred makes him feel unliberal, which makes him feel more guilty, so he spends the rest of the evening "evaluating his motives."

The next day he makes an appointment with his psychiatrist to discuss his hostile feelings against women who demand equal suttee. "Do you think I am still a male chauvinist pig?" he asks, and the psychiatrist replies, "What do you think?" Fifty dollars later, Jonathan leaves the psychiatrist's office with at least three more things to worry about than he had when he went in.

He is too upset to go back to work, so he takes the afternoon off and goes home. His copy of *MS.* has arrived in the mail. Its cover shows a male hand reaching into the blouse of a doll seated at a desk. It is blurbed: "Sexual Harassment in the

Office." Jonathan stares at the cover as he thinks back, evaluating his behavior toward his female co-workers. Has *he* ever wanted to do such a thing? Is that why he did not go back to work after his psychiatric appointment? Was he acting out his guilt by running away from the scene of his unconscious male chauvinism?

When he finishes his *MS.*, which he reads religiously from cover to cover, not skipping anything, he picks up an obscure journal devoted to feminist poetry to which he also subscribes:

MY CUNT   Mine

                                                    I

                                                        tell

                                                            you!

SO KEEP YOUR MOTHER-FUCKING COCK OUT OF

MY CUNT!

The title of this uniambic pentagon is "My Cunt!" Jonathan studies it, carefully weighing its dactyls and anapests, reflecting on how much more relevant it is than "Elaine the fair, Elaine the lovable, Elaine the Lily Maid of Astolat." He reflects so long that before he knows it, it is time to watch "Roots."

That does it. Jonathan can work on his latent male chauvinism but he can't do a thing about being a toubob. "Roots" brings back all the horror of his sixties guilt, before he got into women. With guilt to the right of him and guilt to the left of him, he is now ready to be carried to his shrink's office on a stretcher.

Most Jonathans are too neurotic to be very good in bed, but every now and then a virile Jonathan turns up, chiefly as director of the Little Theater in Back Home, U.S.A., population

90,000. These are the hamlets that are always marked with signs that read: DRIVE SLOWLY, WE LOVE OUR CHILDREN! These signs are sure signs that all the housewives are half-mad and ready for anything. What they get is a Little Theater screw from Jonathan.

The Little Theater screw comes after booze and pills, when a woman, temporarily shriven by her close call with oblivion, enters that stage known as "keeping busy." There are always plenty of other women in the town in the same predicament, so they get together and form a theatrical group in the futile hope that they can bring culture to the Gopher Prairie environment that is driving them wild. There is always some well-meaning but visionary professor emeritus around who makes that standard Woman's Club luncheon speech in which he reminds the ladies that ancient Athens achieved the pinnacle of culture with a population of only 90,000 souls. Therefore, Back Home, U.S.A. can do the same, says the professor, completely forgetting that Plato and Aristotle never cut each other off with, "Hey, the party's getting serious!"

Full of hope, the women import a Little Theater director named Jonathan, who puts on *Private Lives* and picks the most attractive woman in town to play opposite him so that he can lie on top of her in that famous scene. Rehearsals lead inevitably to the Little Theater screw. The woman falls madly in love with Jonathan and they make plans to run away together, but when the day of their planned escape arrives, Jonathan disappears, leaving behind a sorrowful note saying that they can't go on like this, and that he has decided to go back to Cape Cod.

Jonathan leaves a trail of such women all over the country. He also leaves a trail of something else. In one Back Home after another, that timeless speculation makes the rounds: "They say that last child isn't her husband's."

Jonathan can be spotted instantly by that quality of febrile intensity that afflicts chronic imbibers of current events. He lives in a perpetual state of suspense: what will feminists demand next, and will Jonathan be able to give it to them? Obediently, he sees to it that he is all the things that feminists demand that men be: passive, submissive, receptive, emotional, tearful, hysterical—and supportive. When he finds a career woman he turns into a jailer. He will lock her in her atelier if necessary, with the gentle command, "Write, darling, write." Write, paint, sculpt, compose—all of the things that are impossible to do with a mother hen like Jonathan breathing down your neck. He actually believes that if a writer is allotted four hours of "undisturbed" time per day, she will produce X number of pages. He will count them, and he fully expects her to turn out the same number every day. This is how he calculates exactly when she will finish her book. If she does eight pages on Wednesday and only two on Thursday, Jonathan worries: is he being supportive enough? If he does not hear her typewriter clacking steadily behind the locked door, he worries: is his unconscious male chauvinism causing her to have a writing block? Naturally, he is much too considerate to knock and ask if everything is all right, but she *knows* he's there.

A busy woman who is pestered by a supportive man eventually comes to feel the same contempt for him that busy men feel for their helpmate wives. It does not matter who is which sex: the gulf between the doer and the doter can never be bridged. The person who taps softly at a workroom door will become the nemesis of the person behind that door. The supportive person, male or female, kills with kindness, with trays, milk, vitamin pills, and tiptoeing concern, until all they get for their pains is a shout of "Goddamnit!"

Sexual differentiation exists only between the legs. Otherwise, there are people with work temperaments who need to be left alone, and those with love temperaments who need "meaningful relationships" to occupy them. The love people are their own worst enemies because they are invariably drawn to the work people, who come to patronize or despise them. Jonathan is as dependent as Dora Copperfield—and about as helpful.

The creative woman married to a supportive man faces a serious Catch-22. Gavin Lambert describes the irony of Margaret Mitchell's writing career in *The Making of GWTW*:

> She struck her own blow for women's independence, but it was reluctant and painful and would never have been sustained without her husband's help. Fame and fortune, when they arrived, seemed more a threat than a liberation. *She retreated even further into provincial married life and never wrote anything more* (my italics).

Perhaps she had nothing to fight against. The creative urge in women is triggered to a large extent by anger against men. Too many supportive men can spoil the pie.

Like all earnest people, Jonathan has no sense of humor. His profundities can be hilarious, like the one William James uttered when he emerged from his attack of melancholy: "My first act of free will shall be to believe in free will."

Take the matter of liberated English. Only a Jonathan could seriously set forth a plangent encyclical on *te, tes,* and *tir* and call it "The Human Pronoun," as Warren Farrell does in *The Liberated Man.* These humanized gurglings are meant to replace the sexist standard-English pronouns he/she, his/hers, and him/her. He also asks us to call live-in lovers *living persons,* and in what must have been a veritable fit of earnestness he coined *attaché* for spouse.

If he had given any thought to human nature he would have anticipated all the knee-slappers that filled cocktail parties and book review columns the moment his book was published. As a result, the scornful mirth that Farrell brought down around his head ruined what was, on the whole, a very good book. It is impossible to concentrate on it; reading it is like reading very bad galley proofs. By the time I was halfway through it, I had begun to visualize the Human Pronoun as a kind of cartoon character. Betty MacDonald wrote that she always imagined a kilowatt as a hard black peppercorn. I imagine the Human Pronoun as a big fat tear rolling down Warren Farrell's cheek. By the time I finished *The Liberated Man* I was in such a foul mood that I concocted a fantasy in which Farrell is taken prisoner by the Académie Française for calling his wife an *attaché* instead of an *attachée*.

The Académie Française is a rough bunch to cross; I would not want to meet them in a dark alley after missing a pluperfect subjunctive. America needs a similar linguistic watchdog society to protect us from liberated men of both sexes. Meanwhile, let us be grateful that Farrell is not French, else we would have: *"La plume (le stylo) de ma tante (mon oncle)."*

America's Jonathan bears a striking resemblance to England's John Stuart Mill. Mill supported women's rights and wrote extensively on the subject, but his Jonathanoid characteristics are more apparent in another essay, "A Crisis in My Mental History," the famous chapter five of his autobiography.

Next to his lack of humor, and closely connected with it, is Jonathan's other identifying characteristic: his fear of mental illness. All Jonathans have bad nerves because their determined liberality keeps them in a state of intense guilt. Conservative men are crazy to start with, so they can relax and be secure in the knowledge that things cannot possibly get any worse. The liberal man, however, is merely neurotic, so he knows full well that something more is looming out there if he is not careful. It is this fear—not how upset he is but how upset he might become—that runs through Mill's essay.

In true Jonathan fashion, he chooses a calm, pompous title for his tortured screed. "Crisis" is a favorite Jonathan word; it can refer to anything from a race riot to the buzz in his head.

It all started, says Mill, in 1821 when he read Jeremy

Bentham and decided to become a reformer. Until then he had always assumed that happiness was a certainty which he enjoyed by "placing my happiness in something durable and distant, in which some progress might be always making, while it could never be exhausted by complete attainment."

In other words, he could not be happy if he were happy. Here we see the fine Jonathan hand reaching across the page.

For a long time, Mill was happy in this state of delayed happiness, but "in the autumn of 1826" (Jonathan can always pinpoint his crises) things changed.

Mill asked himself; "Suppose that all your objects in life were realized; that all the changes in institutions and opinions which you are looking forward to, could be completely effected at this very instant; would this be a great joy and happiness to you?" The answer, Mill tells us, "was a very distinct NO!"

Jonathan always dreads the day when everybody will agree with him; that future day when everybody is into women, blacks, grape pickers, trees, the whooping crane, the snail darter, and giving the country back to the Indians. How, after all, could Jonathan feel morally superior if everybody else were a Jonathan, too?

Mill: "My heart sank within me: the whole foundation on which my life was constructed fell down. All my happiness was to have been found in the continual pursuit of this end [i.e., happiness]. The end had ceased to charm, and how could there ever again be any interest in the means? I seemed to have nothing left to live for ... my love of mankind, and of excellence for its own sake, had worn itself out."

At this point, Mill himself wore out. He became so exhausted that he took up that standard Jonathan cri de coeur: "The habit of analysis has a tendency to wear away the feelings."

Intellectual though Jonathan is, a part of him hates the intellectual's persona because he believes that thinking is enervating and thus emasculating. In his heart he knows that he is not a good lay, and so from time to time he blames his sexual problems on his tendency to intellectualize everything. "Analysis," said Mill, "is a perpetual worm at the root both of the passions and of the virtues; and above all, fearfully undermines all desires and all pleasures. . . ."

What to do? "The cultivation of the feelings became one of the cardinal points in my ethical and philosophical creed." In other words, Mill, like today's Jonathan, put *cultivate the feelings* on a list of Things to Do. Today's Jonathan would join a touchy-feely encounter group, but Mill turned to music.

However, instead of relaxing and listening to music, Mill started to worry again. Reflecting that the octave consists only of five tones and two semitones which can be put together in only a limited number of ways, he went into another depression:

> It seemed to me that most of these tones must have been already discovered and there could not be room for a long succession of Mozarts and Webers. The pleasure of music fades with familiarity, and requires either to be revived by intermittance, or fed by continual novelty. . . . *I was seriously tormented by the thought of the exhaustibility of musical combinations* (my italics).

We are now ready for that supreme Jonathanoid form of conceit: the conviction that *his* twitch makes the world go round:

> The destiny of mankind in general was ever in my thoughts, and could not be separated from my own. *I felt that the flaw in my life must be a flaw in life itself;* that the question was whether, if the reformers of society and government could succeed in their objects, and every person in the community were free and in a state of physical comfort, the

pleasures of life, being no longer kept up by struggle and privation, would cease to be pleasures. Unless I could see my way to some better hope than this for human happiness in general, my dejection would continue . . . (my italics).

Truly desperate now, Mill resolved to do no more analytical thinking. To relax and calm his frayed nerves, he turned to the rustic poems of Wordsworth.

But no Jonathan can resist analytical thinking for long, no matter how bad an effect it has on him. During Mill's Wordsworth period, he got into an argument with a friend who hated Wordsworth, and so the two of them decided "to have the fight out at our Debating Society, where we accordingly discussed for two evenings the comparative merits of Byron and Wordsworth, propounding and illustrating by long recitations our respective theories of poetry."

Feminists have ordered men to be nurturing, so Jonathan has taken up ecology. When you are having what passes for coitus in his apartment, you must stare at a huge print called *American Bison* on his bedroom wall.

Spending so much time in the psychiatrist's office has robbed Jonathan of the capacity for self-analysis. His motives for joining the ecology movement are a case in point. He tells himself that men, the brutes, are the people who chop down trees and spill oil; therefore he will strike a blow at the male sex by working to prevent such things. He will nurture the wilderness.

In actual fact, he wants the wilderness to nurture him. He is not really interested in ecology; he is merely using the environment as a touchstone with which to regain his lost manhood. The wilderness represents escape from emasculating modern life. He seeks a back-to-nature, Hemingway kind of world in which men can prove their self-sufficiency by coping with life in the raw.

Meanwhile, Jonathan stays home and plays his stereo. His life is fraught with umms and amps and tweeters. His "parts" are his pride and joy and they take up most of the room in his apartment. This is where his power madness comes out; Jonathan is a four-speaker man. He has so much power that he would be evicted if he ever played his stereo without earphones, so he puts them on and lies on the floor in a state of perfect passivity. He cannot hear anything outside his earphones, which is why his landlady is always entering with her passkey and screaming, "Oh, my God, he's dead!"

Jonathan's stereo madness is a case of male chauvinism gone electronic. He gets very smug and impatient whenever a woman does something silly, like calling a needle a needle. "Cartridge!" Jonathan snaps.

There is a perfect way to get his goat. Refer to the entire wall-to-wall mess as "the Victrola."

Another trick of Jonathan's is professional fatherhood. "Fathering" is *the* latest thing, even newer than the clitoris, and Jonathan is into it. He reads all the new books on the joy of male nurturing such as *Tenderness Is Strength* and *Father Feelings* and talks about them constantly. He can be seen in public places planting sudden, passionate kisses on his offspring, who invariably look a little worn.

Jonathan's fathering motives are interesting, too. It is an excellent way for closet male chauvinists to steal some female thunder and reject women at the same time. In the *Newsweek* cover story on "How Men Are Changing," novelist Anne Roiphe makes the ingenuous statement: "I know more and more men who are more involved with their children than with their wives."

Yes, indeed.

6

PAUL CHRISTIAN, ESQ.
or The Misogynist

The standard garden-variety woman hater is easy to spot. My most recent encounter with one occurred in the corridor of a New York hotel. The misogynist always believes that any lone woman in a hotel is either a prostitute or an easy make; it never occurs to him that she might be in New York on business just as he is. My antennae started waving as soon as I saw him coming toward me—woman-haters give off a tangible quality. When we came abreast of each other he gave me a reptilian grin and said, "I'm ready if you are."

I walked on in silence.

"To hell with you then!" he barked after me.

I met another misogynist on a North Carolina horse farm. As I rounded the corner of the stable, a horse that was being led out shied violently. The young man leading it, a scion type in perfectly tailored breeches, snarled: "That's all right, it's nothing but a *woman!*" The expression on his face was like that of the villain in a very bad B movie. His features were "twisted in hatred," as they say in screenplays. Not surprisingly, his attempts to soothe the horse only made it worse. Horses can smell negative human emotions better than any other animal.

Men like this are not the problem, no more than is the dog behind the sturdy fence marked *Beware of Dog*. Forewarned is forearmed; it's the little Pekinese you have to worry about.

The most ubiquitous misogynist is the man with the derisive smile. In *The Descent of Woman*, Elaine Morgan writes: "A man whose gaze is too avidly riveted on a woman's cleavage only gets irritated if he's asked to listen, really listen, to any words coming out of her mouth." Nowadays, most such men know better than to let their irritation show. Instead they suppress it, and then look at the talking woman with a fixed, derisive smile. It is an unmistakable smile of the sort known as "mirthless," the smile of the contemptuous male in the presence of a physically weaker adversary. Bullies smile this way when they pick on someone; they always say, "Don't worry, I'm not going to hurt you," and then they smile that smile. It is the Holocaust smile of the Nazi guard.

Ostensibly civilized men smile this way at women who are too intelligent, too self-assured, too independent. Watch the faces of some male guests—and hosts—on talk shows when a woman guest is holding forth intelligently on a serious subject. The talk show has become the virtual home of misogynistic male smilers because guests are required to talk, and to talk well. The female guest who does her stint properly and fulfills her obligations to be interesting and articulate often finds herself looking at a twitching male mouth.

The talk show has become one of the chief carriers of misogyny—the media's answer to Typhoid Mary. Although it is supposed to suggest a sophisticated mixed-company group of friends sitting around in someone's living room, it comes off more like a bull session or a fraternity meeting thanks to the self-consciously boyish types who have cornered the host market. Except for living legends like Bette Davis, any female guest who has enjoyed the benefits of evolution longer than Charo or Dody Goodman seems to spark male hostility.

A foremost woman hater is the man who talks too much about loyalty and demands that women prove their loyalty to him.

There are times in a woman's life when she ought to say, "Get thee behind me, Satan," but she never does. Instead she "sticks by her man" as they say in country music songs. This is the philosophy of the gun moll, and it leads to moral death. It can start in little ways. The woman who breaks a dinner engagement with another woman because a man calls at the last minute and asks her for a date is practicing the most innocuous form of stick-by-your-man. Most women have done that, and the other woman usually understands, but that is not the point. A broken word is a broken word, and it is *wrong*, no matter who understands. The process of demoralization has begun, and a man was the cause of it all.

When I was in college, one of my sorority sisters was going steady with a boy who had signed up for Survey of English Literature, which I had taken the previous year. The textbook was extremely expensive, so my sorority sister asked me if I would lend mine to her boyfriend. I did, but at the end of the term he did not return it. Finally I asked him for it, but he denied that he had ever borrowed it. I went to my sorority sister and told her what he had said. "I gave it to him that day in the coffee shop while you were there," I said. "Don't you remember?" No, she did not remember. She had never asked me to lend him the book. He had bought his own copy; she was with him when he bought it. She stuck by her man.

Such men, resenting the moral superiority that men themselves have forced women to adopt, are compelled to try to corrupt us. They simply have a blind need to make a woman do something wrong, especially if it will benefit them. Their chief weapon is an appeal to loyalty. Women, they sigh, do not know the meaning of the word. Women are disloyal by nature—look at Delilah and Cressida, both of them symbols of treachery. You can't trust a woman; no woman will hang in there when the going gets rough. Women are fair-weather friends, and ad infinitum. Enough of this browbeating and a woman will cave in and commit a reprehensible act simply to prove that she is "not like the others." Sometimes she will even commit a mortal sin. The Manson girls vied with each other to prove who was the most loyal to the master. Bonnie Parker stuck by her man, and so did Myra Hindley, who helped Ian Brady kill three children in England's "Moors Murders."

There need not be an intimate relationship between a man and his female accomplice. The secretary who juggles the books or perjures herself for her boss is practicing stick-by-your-man. Secretaries are notorious zombies and so are nurses because their jobs require an especially airtight "loyalty oath" to the masculine mystique.

The murderer of women—who is obviously a misogynist—depends heavily on female loyalty to the masculine mystique. It was "The Master's Voice" that made the Boston Strangler's victims open their doors to him when he announced that the landlord had sent him to fix the plumbing. All too many women cannot say no to a man who claims he has come to help or improve or fix, especially when he demands entrance in the name of another man. The Strangler's victims *knew* they had not complained of leaky pipes or broken toilets, but their loyalty to the male as problem solver was too strong. Men know best, so they let him in.

While I was still susceptible to the masculine mystique I did things that I would not do now. A lover who did my 1957 income tax persuaded me to deduct cigarette taxes, although I did not then smoke, and gasoline taxes, although I did not drive. It went against my grain but I let him do it because he made me feel that it was my *duty* to trust him. As I signed my name to the tax form, he chuckled and said, "It's our secret." I looked up and into his eyes, and saw in them a victorious glee, and behind the glee, something as cold as marble.

The loyalty demander also exploits woman's eternal fear of seeming to be Miss Goody Two Shoes. Women are afraid to exhibit any form of puritanism in front of a man for fear it will rub off on our sexual image. He implies that if a woman will not cheat or steal or perjure herself, she is probably uptight in bed, too. His talent for moral alchemy is such that he can equate larceny and embezzlement with sixty-nine or a cheek squeeze. He can confuse a woman so much that she will end up doing all four.

A classic misogynist is the man who is convinced that inside every woman lurks a feral houri known as "a real woman." Bringing this genie out of the bottle becomes a prime test of his masculinity, and he will stop at nothing.

Mary McCarthy has such a man in her novel *A Charmed Life.* His name is Sandy Gray and his victim is Dolly Lamb, a rich young spinster who paints.

Dolly, to paraphrase her creator, is a scrubbed, shining, cool-as-a-cucumber girl who never has a hair out of place. Industrious even in her pleasures, she reminds people of a sober little girl making mud pies. She is so prim that when she recites the lines of a tragic heroine at a play reading, she sounds like an imperturbable senior prefect in a boarding school reporting to the headmistress.

Dolly is ladylike, virginal, and happy with her work, even though her art teachers have faulted her painting for its "timid conceits, quaint charm, and meticulous craftsmanship." But Dolly knows that these qualities are part of her personality, so sensibly she decides that art and self are well integrated. She is painting what she feels and what she is.

She meets Sandy Gray, a former art editor and "a rusticated bohemian, solemn and loquacious and self-vaunting, a not-very-intelligent and pretentious bore." Sandy enters Dolly's house uninvited, stares in disgust at her pretty still life—a bowl of mushrooms—then he picks it up and heaves it out the door, calling it "corrupt and dainty."

Next he sneers at her neat little collection of shells and starfish that she has arranged in a carefully graduated series on her mantle. "Stop hoarding," he tells her. "It's your own shit you're assembling there, in neat, constipated little packages."

Dolly, who hates coarse language, blushes. Sandy smiles and asks her challengingly: "Are you shocked?" When she nods mutely he instructs: "You mustn't be shocked by anything. That's the first lesson for the artist."

Now he is ready to criticize her painting. He hates it, he tells her; it makes him want to "spew."

Her work was sick, he told her—cramped with preciosity and mannerisms. Underneath, he discerned talent, but it was crippled, like some poor tree tortured out of shape by a formal gardener. She needed to be bolder and freer.

Dolly has heard this many times before from her art teachers.

But it wearied and confused her to be assured that there was a vital force imprisoned inside her that was crying to be let out. . . . If there was anybody else inside her . . . it was a creature still more daunted and mild and primly scrupulous than the one the world saw.

Hurt and insulted, Dolly starts to cry, but Sandy offers her that ultimate misogynistic consolation: someday she will be a *real* woman.

They embark upon a relationship that is supported chiefly by

Dolly's money while she obediently strives for the passionate, elemental breakthrough in her work that Sandy urges on her. The results are discouraging.

When she "let herself go," her paintings got big and mechanical; she painted drearily, in the style of the teacher who had advised her to be herself. She was tired, moreover, of being told she had talent. She had come to feel that it was like a disease.

In the end of the novel, we find a new, bold, elemental Dolly whose breakthrough—and breakdown—are now complete.

Dolly looked badly, very peaked and worn. Her little breasts seemed sunken under her pale-blue shirt and black sweater. Her eyes were sunk back, too, and that bright, inflamed look, as though she had just been crying or having her cheeks scrubbed by an angry nursegirl, had become almost too real. . . . Dolly should have been outside painting, but she stood, hugging herself by the stove, with a lackluster air, like a shut-in. Her collections of seashells and fish skeletons had been dismantled; a bunch of cattails stood awry in a milk bottle. The sun's rays showed crumbs on the table. In the kitchen, through the open door, Martha could see a gallon jug, half empty, of the cheapest white California. A slight smell of wine was noticeable on Dolly's breath.

The morale-destroyer misogynist is often an intellectual who hates his own sexual desires because they interfere with his powers of concentration. Misery loves company, so if he can bring out "the real woman" in a woman, he has equalized the situation. By encouraging a woman to free the beast within her, he is actually encouraging her to destroy her career. A houri is not likely to get much work done; if he can unearth an elemental passion in a woman, he can accomplish, in effect, what less complicated misogynists call "keeping her barefoot and pregnant."

Men have always resented the ease with which women can have sexual intercourse. All we have to do is be present. We do not have to be aroused, we do not even have to be conscious, and to carry it to the grim end, we do not even have to be alive. Such effortless participation in an act that requires so much of the male is bound to cause a certain amount of envy in every man. In the severely neurotic man, such envy leads to hatred.

This is the On and On and On Misogynist whose invariable sweet nothing is: "You women can go on and on and on, can't you?" Unlike the selfish mysogynist, who rolls over and goes to sleep afterward, the On and On and On boy always sits up immediately on the edge of the bed and lights a cigarette. There is a deadly silence for several minutes, broken only by the scrape of the match and the first long, labored inhalation. Then comes the *puck!* as he snatches the cigarette out of his lips and hunches over, elbows on knees. He sits as far away from you as he can get, usually on the very edge of the bed—a position that caused naked men untold woe back in the days of wire bedsprings.

He must prove that you are incapable of *something*, so he frames negative questions like, "I don't suppose you have a Coke or something."

You get him that Coke, and he drinks it in silence while perched on the edge of the mattress. He stays like that for so long that any woman who was raised to be a good hostess— which is just about every woman—starts to worry about his comfort, so she says: "Don't you want to lie down?"

At last he turns around.

"You ready for another session? You women can go on and on and on, can't you?"

There is a little bit of On and On and On in every man. The male tendency to confuse the female's capacity to be penetrated with her desire to be penetrated is nowhere more in evidence than early in the morning, when men are afflicted with what they fondly refer to as a "piss hard-on."

I believe in reincarnation but I do not believe there is life before noon.

Self-appointed sexperts have created a new kind of misogynist especially for the seventies. This is the man who has been singing "Anything You Can Do I Can Do Better" ever since the first time he saw a girl throw a baseball. He hasn't sung a note since the theory of multiple orgasms was promulgated.

The multiple-orgasm sexperts remind me of the greedy grandmother in the mini-ravioli commercial who counts in her own favor: "One for you, and one-two-three for me." I suspect that the sexperts, knowing they were writing in a pro-female era, saw the wisdom and cash value of counting in women's favor. The result has created an uproar in a nation that was already on the verge of sexual hysteria to begin with. Magazines rushed into the fray with The-Truth-About article and sexual advice forums filled up with letters from desperate men asking: "How can I tell if this chick I'm balling has multiple orgasms?"

Men who used to raise themselves up on their elbows immediately afterward and pant, "Did you?" now pant, "How many?" The specter of the female's infinite capacity has now become more infinite and more spectral. If multiple orgasm were a French verb tense it would be called *Plus-Que-Parfait Superlatif.* Nothing less will do now, and everybody is conjugating like mad in an attempt to achieve what the sexperts have told them they should achieve—and have a *right* to expect. It would not be such a serious problem if America were not a Christian country, but when hucksterism sets women up as all-powerful goddesses within a religious framework that has no goddesses, it creates frightened, hate-filled men. Greek and Roman pagans of old could have taken the multiple-orgasmic woman in their stride—after all, they had Aphrodite and Venus. The closest thing to a female deity in America is the Virgin Mary. The theory of the multiple orgasm has created a miracle gap that is fast filling up with misogynists.

I am as confused as everyone else on this subject. I don't know whether I have had multiple orgasms or not. There is a second series of much-diminished throbs that comes after the big flurry, but I think this is just the female version of detumescence. I certainly have never had twenty or thirty, unless you want to count each throb as a separate orgasm. I have a sneaking suspicion that the sexperts have done just that: one for men, and one-two-three for women. In any case, the controversy has created confused lovers, and confused lovers are hostile lovers.

Even the words "multiple orgasm" have begun to sound hostile when a man says them. I prefer the more affectionate "snapping pussy."

There is a certain kind of misogynist who hates all orgasmic women. He can control his hatred with a woman who is frigid or complacent, but like Coach Popper in Larry McMurtry's novel *The Last Picture Show*, he gets furious the moment she starts to move. He may pull out and finish on her stomach, and afterward say something unforgivable, like Coach Popper's: "I always heard that women got nasty when they got older."

This is the classic stud who lives in dread of being used as a stud by women. His psychology is revealed in a passage in James Jones' novel *The Merry Month of May*:

You take a woman and . . . bring her on toward coming . . . and before long, you reached a point where you ceased to exist as you for her . . . became just a man, any man, who is giving her excitation.... Carry it a while further and you ceased to be even a man, and became some object, some thing which is causing her to have pleasure. Carry it on all the way to where she comes and you ceased even to be an object. Because in the midst of her come nothing exists except herself and what she's feeling ... what you've done is "stimulate" yourself right out of existence.

The Pietropinto and Simenauer Misogynist is not new, but now he has been collected in one volume. The authors of *Beyond the Male Myth* proudly point out that their survey contained "a high representation of middle-class and upper-class men," and then proceed to give their readers samples of the thoughts of these scions. In the chapter devoted to what turns men off, we can contemplate these privileged communications:

"Swanky walk, nose in the air, tone of voice, New England accent burn me up."

"Some snooty cunt who's too good for you."

"A big ass turns me off most."

"Body proportions out of align."

The brutish misogynist is the man who takes any form of female refinement as a personal snub. It is for him that low-level girlie magazines run photos of nearly nude women in garter belts with twisted, baggy black stockings. He demands flaws in women, and if he doesn't get them he flies into a murderous rage.

He is the man who calls internal fondling "playing stink-finger," yet at the same time he is berating women for olfactory vileness, he is simultaneously on the lookout for what he calls "eating pussy." The woman who fits this category is the woman of obvious refinement and flawless grooming. The moment he sees her, he does his best to insult and embarrass her with loud remarks about her snootiness and the angle of her nose.

His woman hatred is actually class hatred. The brutish misogynist lives in a sexual time capsule, too. It is labeled circa 1900, when his patriarchal wife-beating grandfather got a job digging ditches at a dollar a day. Grandfather had many opportunities to watch the "real ladies" strolling downtown to shop, and he never forgot them. Neither has the brutish misogynistic grandson. His conflicting obsessions with vaginal odors and cunnilingus go back to the days when only upper-class women had the means to bathe daily. The woman who is "eating pussy" is still his class enemy.

Feminists of the Madame De Farge persuasion have done their part to create misogynists out of normally genial men. Women who scream "Creep!" at the top of their lungs when a man merely winks at them on the street, or "Get your mother-fuckin' hands off me!" in elevators and subways may feel better for it, but they leave a trail of seething men behind them. The perpetrator of the goose or the pinch deserves to be shaken up, but the decibel level of the Madame De Farge feminist reaches the ears of many, many perfect gentlemen as well. It is these men who have started to do a slow boil.

The both-barrels response to importuning men has frequently been the subject of feminist authors and of reader mail in feminist magazines. Last year *MS.* ran an article on how to walk alone on the street by a woman who had lived for a time in Greece, where respectable women must keep their eyes downcast to avoid incident. The article drew a memorable letter-to-the-editor from a woman who had discovered the perfect way to handle an attempted pickup. Luckily, she was afflicted with chronic asthma or catarrh or something that kept her plugged up with phlegm. Whenever a man approached her, she cleared her throat, brought up a lump of mucus, and spat.

Similar feminist recommendations that I have read include producing a bowel movement if a man tries to rape you. The theory behind all such recommendations is that men are disgusted by stark evidence of woman's physical functions, so the wise woman will protect herself by disgusting them even more. Men do harbor a certain pristine ideal, which is why reading such recommendations makes them angry. A kick in the groin, however much it hurts, is still a compliment of sorts because it says, in effect, that a man has something to kick. On the other hand, a shower of feces or vomit says, in effect, that he is a toilet.

The Madame De Farge feminists have forgotten, if indeed they ever knew, that rude men shrivel easily, like snails doused with salt. The sledgehammer will never replace the rapier in woman's battle for the last word. I shall never forget an exchange I once overheard. The man said, "I wish I had a little pussy" and the woman replied, "So do I, mine's as big as a bucket."

I would give ten years off my life if I could have been the one who said it.

An infallible clue to the misogynist is his inability to bring off a bawdy remark with élan and affection. Most feminists seem determined to destroy the nonmisogynistic man's sexual humor. In the July 1978 issue of *MS.*, the "No Comment" department, which I consider the only consistently readable part of the magazine, featured an anecdote that appeared in *The Stars and Stripes* newspaper:

Why mothers' milk is better than cows' milk:
1. It keeps fresh longer.
2. You can take it to picnics.
3. The cat can't get at it.
4. It comes in such cute containers.

I found this delightful. I also enjoyed my gynecologist's explanation of why he repaired a short circuit in his office instead of calling an electrician: "A conductor tube is a conductor tube. If you can fix one, you can fix 'em all."

Neither do I object to *broad* if it is used in a nonhostile way. It usually is. Men often used it as a term of jaunty endearment until feminists launched their sexist language campaign and drove jaunty men underground. Now *broad* has become a men's washroom word. Like most women, I find *cunt* completely unacceptable in most situations, but it has its place in lascivious private moments and in erotic love letters. One of my favorite sex words, which lends itself to a great deal of tenderness when spoken by the right kind of man, is *twat* but it seems to have gone underground, too.

At the same time feminists have been washing men's mouths out with soap, they have cheered so-called liberated women for their brave new use of *fuck* in their speech and writings. When men use *fuck* they are chauvinist pigs, but when women use it they are liberated. That's feminist logic, and it makes men understandably furious.

If feminists keep pounding away at male ribaldry, we will never again have another Shakespeare or Chaucer. We *will* have lots of resentful men, afraid to open their mouths around women, who retreat to all-male enclaves like the washroom to practice their ribaldry. Ribaldry never lasts long in the men's room; it quickly degenerates into simple dirty talk—the supreme mark of the misogynist.

7

JENNIE KICKED ME
or Men You Love
to Hate

Somerset Maugham wrote: "There is no cruelty greater than a woman's to a man who loves her and whom she does not love; she has no kindness then, no tolerance even, she has only an insane irritation."

The Human Bondage man is always such a *nice* man, but the nicer he is, the more hell he catches. He is the man who inspires that immortal female line, "If you don't stop doing that, I'm going to scream!" *That* can be just about anything. Anna Karenina threatened to scream whenever her husband cracked his knuckles. Scarlett O'Hara flew into a fit whenever Frank Kennedy clicked his tongue. The man who clears his throat tentatively before speaking always triggers an apoplectic reaction in women.

The lowest boiling point in American fiction belongs to Leda March, the heroine of Nancy Hale's novel *The Prodigal Women*. When it comes to lighting into men, Leda is an upper-class Boston version of Maugham's cockney waitress, Mildred. Leda is engaged to her cousin, James March. Shortly before the wedding, they are seated in the garden, when James happens to say that after they are married, he is going to be an "uxorious fellow." That does it . . .

"What do you mean, uxorious?"

"Uxorious means wife-loving, darling."

"I know what it means. But if you mean wife-loving, why don't you say wife-loving?"

"I sort of like uxorious. It's a nice word."

"I can't bear pomposity."

"Don't get mad at me, darling. I didn't mean anything."

"I'm not mad at you!"

"I know, I know, darling. It's been awfully hot, and of course it is a strain for you."

"*What* is a strain for me?"

"Well, the emotional strain we are both bound to be under while we are engaged."

"Oh, don't be *loathsome!*"

"Darling, darling, don't be nervous. Everything's all right. I'll be so sweet to you. Everything will be lovely when we get all this folderol over and are alone together."

"Please don't say alone together."

"I won't say anything."

Merely thinking about James' sterling qualities makes Leda furious.

He had not asked her to marry him, but she knew that he was going to; sometimes she felt the wildest irritation from her very knowledge of his intentions. . . . Already she had lived through the moment of his proposal a dozen times, and turned hot with exasperation, and thrown back at him a variety of stinging dismissals. She had said "I loathe the very sound of your idiotic voice," and "What made you ever think that I would marry a Bostonian fool like yourself?" . . . Leda leaned her head back on the seat cushion in an attempt to relax; she was tingling with irritation ... she wished she could hurt him. She wished she knew someone evil, whom she could prefer to James, to show him that his loving-kindness was really the most cloying stupidity. She would like to shock him, to outrage him; not from any desire to sin but only to explain to him how boring he was. . . . Sometimes she thought that she might be able to feel attracted to him if he could once tell her of something really wrong that he had done. But it was all so virtuous, honorable, boring ... those gentle eyes, that considerateness; there was nothing in him that caught her breath. . . .

The best scene in Henry Morton Robinson's novel *The Cardinal* is the one in which Mona Fermoyle and Emmett Burke go to the movies. As they leave the theater, Mona looks with bitter scorn at Emmett, noting his "breathlets, his speckled neckties, his weekly haircuts." She thinks to herself: "If he talks about firing pins tonight I'll throw his three-sixteenths carat diamond on the sidewalk and stamp on it." When Emmett suggests a banana split, Mona "wanted to smash his new round hat over his ears, and run shrieking down the street."

Poor Emmett cannot understand why Mona is so quiet, so to break the silence and cheer her up, he talks all the way home:

Down the tree-shaded vista of Maple Street he spoke of the new pool table the K of C had just installed. Passing lilacs in bloom, he described a tenth-inning rally that the Red Sox had made last Saturday in Cleveland. The blue arch light at the corner of Highland Avenue blinked unpityingly down on a stocky young man trying to explain the bolt-action of a Springfield rifle to a slender young woman. . . . Crunching up the gravelly walk ... Emmett furtively popped a Sen-Sen into his mouth, in preparation for the goodnight kiss.

That night, Mona runs away from home and becomes the mistress of a Spanish white slaver.

I had a Human Bondage beau when I was twenty. My father referred to him as "poor Jim" because he was always carrying heavy packages and foot lockers for me, and driving me around town. Poor Jim worshiped the ground I walked on, although I walked more on him than I walked on the ground. I got mad at poor Jim when we saw *Gone With the Wind* solely because he was not like Rhett Butler. As I watched the famous scene in which Scarlett is carried upstairs, I felt Maugham's "insane irritation" stirring in me.

"If you don't stop rattling that popcorn I'm going to scream!"

"I'm sorry," said poor Jim.

After the show, we went to the Hot Shoppe for a snack.

"I'm going to *scream* if you don't stop tapping your fingers!"

"I'm sorry."

"If you say I'm sorry one more time ..."

"I'm sor—all right, I won't say it, I promise."

"You put four spoonfuls of sugar in that coffee. Why do you have to use so much sugar!"

"I love sweet things—that's why I love you."

"Oh, shut *up!*"

What makes Jennie kick nice men? In her essay "The Pernicious Effects of Women's Mis-education," the world's first feminist, Mary Wollstonecraft, wrote that because women are "rendered giddy by the whole tenor of their lives, the very aspect of wisdom or the severe graces of virtue must have a lugubrious appearance to them. . . . How can they be expected to relish in a lover what they do not, or very imperfectly, possess themselves?"

A woman can easily come to hate a nice man because his kindness, patience, and passivity are the very qualities that the world demands of her. His niceness reminds us of the nice roles we are forced to play. Nice men, in short, are us. We are really kicking ourselves.

Even more irritating than the nice man is Saint Michael the Good. The Michael Man is the unexciting prize catch that old ladies try to foist on young ladies. Michael is a most suitable name for him. A good, solid, respectable name; strong without being macho, sober and serious without being *too* stuffy, and biblical enough to suggest a vague purity. Michael is also a fine middle-of-the-road name guaranteed to offend no one because it belongs to everyone. It is Jewish—the Hebraic spelling is strikingly obvious when we stop and really look at it—and yet it is also Irish. However, it's neither Jewish nor Irish, but thoroughly American. Just as Patricia is an all-American name now, instead of the feminine of Patrick, Michael has made it into the apple-pie league, too. Michael is such a standard, dependable name that even fortune-tellers have found a use for it. In Gail Parent's novel *David Meyer Is a Mother*, the con artist clairvoyant warns, "Beware of Michael!" She realized that everyone knows lots of Michaels, so she couldn't miss.

There is nothing wrong with Michael. In fact, there is everything right with him. He is good-looking without being too handsome, intelligent without being dazzling or overbearing, well bred and well educated. He has a good job, a good future, a good disposition, good health, good teeth, and good arches. He is the type that hostesses of yesteryear meant when they said, "Bring your young man," because you can take Michael anywhere. He is also the "extra man" that every hostess craves, which is why every woman has a Michael story.

Michael is clean-cut, well dressed, honorable, patient, articulate, kind, brave, reverent, and punctual. I have only one objection to Michael: I CAN'T STAND HIM!

Life with Michael is one long guilt trip. A woman finds herself thinking: "He's so kind, decent . . . why can't I like him? Any woman who was honorable, patient, kind, brave, and reverent would like Michael, but I don't. There must be something wrong with me. Any woman who does not like Michael has no future, only a past. Any girl who does not like Michael must have bad teeth and fallen arches. In short, any woman who does not like Michael must be a terrible person. Therefore, I am a terrible person."

The guilt problem is always made worse by older women, who invariably adore Michael. In *Looking For Mr. Goodbar*, an older woman introduces Theresa Dunn to James Morrisey, "every Irish mother's favorite son. Pink, smooth-faced, well behaved. Hairless. Neat as a pin." The older woman takes Theresa into the kitchen for one of those inevitable summit meetings in which she extols James' many virtues in a testimonial that begins: "He's a wonderful boy." James' father died when he was very young. James applied nose to grindstone, worked his way through school, and now is the sole support of his crippled mother. James has had a very hard life; at one point he even peddled books door-to-door. He's really a wonderful boy.

At this stage in Theresa's tormented life, the very last thing she needed to complete her self-hatred was a Michael Man, but that is what she got. The burden of James Morrisey's sterling character, especially when compared to her own very different one, provoked a rebellion in her that made her step up her bar-hopping, which led to her murder.

I was set up for Michael-guilt long before I met my first Michael. I grew up hearing paeans and eulogies to that vessel of male purity that Victorian women called a Good Man. Such a man was my grandfather. I never knew him and I was very glad I had not, because Granny made him sound like a cross between Anthony Comstock and the Pharisees. He was in the army around the turn of the century and was stationed in Kansas, which is how he happened to be in one of the saloons that Carry Nation hit. However: "Your grandfather never touched a drop of liquor in his life. The reason he was in the saloon was to check on his men to see that they weren't drinking too much. Why, if anybody put a drink in front of him, he would push it away."

"The only time he ever pushed away a drink was when it had too much water in it," said my mother, but Granny ignored her.

The Inconsolable Widow was one of Granny's favorite roles, and she played it to the hilt each time we visited my grandfather's grave. Trailing shawls and veils, she swept grandly into the plot and sank down on the ledge, a delicately embroidered handkerchief at her eyes.

"He was such a good man," she began in a tremulous voice. "He never raised his voice, never. Not in all the years we were married. A perfect gentleman. Every time I entered the room he stood up. I never heard a swearword pass his lips. He was so *good* to me! Whatever I wanted, all I had to do was ask him. And the children, too. He set such a good example for them. He never touched tobacco."

"He rolled his own Bull Durhams," said my mother, but Granny went on without a pause.

"He was a prince among men! The day for such men is past, we won't see his like again. There were giants in the earth in those days."

Away from the cemetery, and when I got a little older, she hinted at another virtue beloved by Victorian wives. "He was so considerate. He never *bothered* me too often," she would whisper, with significant movements of her eyebrows.

During my dreamy high school days, she tried her best to

stamp out my romanticism and replace it with a good, solid realistic appreciation of the Good Man. The conversation we had the day I finished reading *On the Eve* was typical.

"It's about an aristocratic Russian girl named Elena and her dying lover!" I effused. "He's Insarov."

"Is that what ails him?"

"No, Granny, it's his *name!* He's a revolutionary."

"Well, she'd better watch her P's and Q's around him if she's an aristocrat. Look what those Communists did to that nice Czar and his sweet family. Took that little girl down in the cellar and shot her full of holes. But they say she's still alive somewhere. They're saving her money for her in a Swiss bank."

"Anyhow," I cut in, "Insarov has TB."

"Consumption?" Granny said, her eyes lighting with interest. "Does he die in the end?"

"Yes, and—"

"Does she catch it?"

"No! Will you let me finish? Elena loves him so much that she takes him to Italy and stays with him until he dies. After that, she's so heartbroken that she becomes a nurse in the Crimean War. She decides to sacrifice herself."

"Does she catch another husband?"

"Of course not! She's hearbroken."

"That heart will mend mighty fast after she picks off a few lice and empties a few bedpans. You mean to tell me she was right smack in the middle of the whole Russian army and she didn't find another husband? She could have had her pick."

"Dat right," said Emma, putting in her two cents. "She oughta git her some nice awficer gent'man. Dey gits a pension."

"But she was in love with Insarov!"

"She could fall in love with somebody else if she tried. Besides, for a woman, love comes after marriage. The important thing is to find a good man you can respect."

"You listen to yo' Big Momma. She tellin' it."

By this time, Emma had been widowed, too, so I had to listen to *her* eulogy to *her* Good Man.

"He nebber waste his money, nosiree! He brung his pay envelope home to me wid de flap still glued down. De other mens, dey usta say, 'Charlie, c'mon play some poker, jes' a penny a hand,' but he say no, he dint gamble none, he take his pay home to his wife and chillern."

"That's right," Granny said. "Charlie was so good."

I looked at the two of them in disbelief. I distinctly remembered the day Charlie bet the tires on his employer's truck in a poker game. They played four hands and Charlie lost all four tires, one by one. When he came home, Emma chased him down the alley with a broom, yelling, "I'll whup yo' tail till yo' nose bleed buttermilk!"

Now that Charlie was dead, Emma had rewritten history in the classic Granny manner. I gave up and left the room, feeling vaguely guilty for remembering something bad about this Good Man.

My first Michael Man entered my life when I was twenty-one. He was everything a girl could wish for, though he looked a bit like a tall, well-built owl in his black horn-rims. He confessed to me that his vision was 20/20, but that he wore window-glass spectacles to look more serious and substantial to his boss.

Michaels are always well rounded. Mine was a CPA who sang tenor in a choral group in his spare time, a fact that provided my father, who couldn't stand him, with his famous prediction: "If you marry him, some night you'll wake up and say, 'Michael, for God's sake sing!' "

Men often see through Michaels, but old ladies never do. Michael snowed Granny. Granny snowed Michael. It was the most nauseating mutual admiration society I have ever witnessed. I heard nothing but Michael, Michael, Michael. Every night at dinner, Granny reminded me that Michael had "prospects."

"He'll be a good provider, you'll never want for anything. He's so *steady*. He told me he goes to bed at eleven on the dot every night so he can get up early and study accounting bulletins. He'll be a good influence on you, stop you from running around like a night-crawling insect. After all the trash I've seen wander through this house, I never thought you'd have sense enough to bring home a good man. Mark my words, if you don't marry Michael you'll die on the vine. You'll never catch another beau like him. They broke the mold when they made Michael."

"That's why he's so moldy," said my father.

If I had been closer to my father, I could have derived strength from his attitude, but Granny had always ruled our roost by divine right, so it was her opinions that mattered to me. I felt obligated to fall in love with Michael, so I kept going out with him. After all, he was a Good Man; if I gave him a chance, I would eventually see his worth.

Most of the time, all I saw were *two* Michaels. He bored me so much that I had to get drunk whenever I was with him. The euphoria that resulted made me seem to be having a much better time than I actually was having, which encouraged Michael to think that perhaps I was falling in love with him. Five highballs made me sufficiently affectionate so that I could forget, for an hour or so, that I was with Michael. The next day, I would sink into remorse.

As I sat at the kitchen table nursing my headaches, Granny would come in beaming like a procuress and demand chapter and verse about the previous evening. What did Michael say? What *exactly* did he say? Did you walk past Galt's Jewelers? Did he stop and look at the rings?

"Granny, please," I groaned.

"You shouldn't drink so much with Michael. He told me that

he never has more than *one*. You'd never catch *him* making a spectacle of himself. No man likes a woman who drinks more than he does, especially a serious man like Michael. He wouldn't stand for a wife who was a toper, no indeed, not Michael."

It was partly to get away from Michael that I went away to graduate school. Women are always going to graduate school or taking the Foreign Service exam to get away from the Michael Man. The most oppressive thing about him is his vine-covered-cottage philosophy. He firmly believes that every woman wants to marry and settle down. He reasons that if he waits long enough—and he is a font of patience—you will get tired of your job and fall into his arms. He lurks in the wings of a woman's life in the hope of catching her in a weak moment and "taking her away from it all."

His strategy is basically sound. Women *do* get tired of jobs. In the fifties especially, one hour on a typical "woman's job" was enough to cause an attack of the screaming meemies. Being a *Gal Fri with a smile in your voice, lite typing* was even worse than being married to Michael. I was afraid I would cave in and marry him, so I went off to Ole Miss for a grand and glorious Michael-less year of tourist cabins, Coca-Cola douches, and armed and dangerous bootleggers.

Granny deplored my decision. "You'll never find another Michael," she mourned. She was wrong.

The typical Michael Man can easily get to be a habit because he has a fiendish tendency to turn up when there are no other men in a woman's life. The instant she meets him she knows he is a Michael, but she ignores the warning bells and tells herself: "It can't hurt to have dinner with him." This decision marks the beginning of the end.

Michael is *so* nice at dinner, so solicitous of her every wish, that she cannot bring herself to say no the next time he asks her out. It would be terrible to hurt him. The fact that Michael is not sexually aggressive gets her in deeper because she tells herself: "It can't hurt to see him once in a while on a casual basis."

Michael usually has money and he is a liberal spender, so eventually his new lady friend starts to feel guilty. To repay him, she invites him to dinner at her apartment, telling herself: "After all, there's nothing wrong with cooking dinner for a casual friend."

It is here that Michael starts to take root. He is so humbly grateful for the dinner you cooked for him, so lavish in his praise of your culinary talents, that you cannot say no the next time he asks you out.

The game is afoot. There is now a Michael in your life, and you aren't sure how he got there. There is also a Michael in your bed, which is even more puzzling, because Michael does not "set fire to a woman's haystack," as Lady Chatterley's bawdy Scottish father put it. He is so damned considerate! Feminists get incensed when anyone says that a woman wants a man to treat her roughly, but whenever Michael gave me his tender smile and murmured his "Shall we make love?" I started to think longingly of the Earl of Bothwell, Marcus Agrippa, Hotspur, and Alaric the Goth. Even worse are Michael's sexual invitations when he is in what is, for him, a roguish mood. With a devastating arc of his eyebrow, he asks: "You weren't by any chance planning to take a sleeping pill tonight, were you?"

The first time I went to bed with Michael, he said: "Tell me what you like." It never occurs to him that he ought to find out for himself. Every time he touches an erogenous zone he asks, "Here?" Afterward he asks, "Did you?" He has no gift for tender ribaldry; he would never say "come" or "climax." When he is feeling even more considerate than usual he will ask: "Did I make you happy?" and worse, "Did I bring you happiness?" It's like sleeping with a greeting card.

Enough of this and a woman longs to shock Michael down to his Peel's Ltd. wing tips. I started saying things like: "When I worked at Big Lily's, the rule was one towel to a customer," to which Michael replied, "Now, now," accompanied by an indulgent little chuckle that got more nerve-wracking every time I heard it.

Michael brings out a quality of fey desperation in women. Whenever I was with him, I had the wildest urges to jump into a fountain, imitate King Kong, or simulate an epileptic fit in the theater lobby. I restrained myself, which brought on an even wilder frustration, which led inevitably to a severe depression.

The Michael depression is like none other. I felt as though I weighed a thousand pounds. I could not get out of bed. The mere thought of washing out a bra was exhausting. Straightening the bookshelves was comparable to the labors of Hercules. I lay in bed waiting for Michael's daily phone call, dreading the sound of his considerate voice saying, "Am I disturbing you?" I felt as if I were drowning in the Sea of Michael. I tried to masturbate but I was so tired I couldn't "lift a finger," as fragile Southern women say. Besides, every time I got Mario Lanza or Stewart Granger fleshed out in my fantasy, Michael's considerate face rose up in my mind, blotting out my dream men. I curled up in a fetal position and studied the sliver of gravel embedded in my right knee, a souvenir of a 1942 race across the playground. Masochistically—to punish myself for not liking Michael the Good—I tried to cut out the gravel with a nail file. Just then the phone rang.

"Am I disturbing you?"

"No, I was just cutting out the gravel in my knee."

"Now, now."

That did it. All the other things I had said to shock him were lies, but this was true. There *is* a piece of gravel in my knee. The scales fell from my eyes, followed by the guilt from my shoulders. Michael was *not* nice, he only appeared to be. Because he was not sexually aggressive, the only way he could capture a woman was by burrowing in her life like a tick in a dog's ear.

The Michael spell was broken. The next day, I quit my job, put everything in storage, emptied my savings account, and went to Paris.

Once in a great while, the Michael Man gets mad at himself for being so kind and considerate and decides to play the aggressive, dominant male. On these momentous occasions, he dispenses with his usual, "Shall we make love?" and says instead, "Come here, you little fool!"

It never works. There is nothing to do but laugh in his face.

The He-Goat Man is an extremely heavy cross for women to bear. His attitude is expressed in a fable by Aesop:

> The she-goats, having obtained of Jupiter the favor of a beard, the he-goats, full of concern, began to be indignant that the females rivaled them in their dignity. "Suffer them," said the God, "to enjoy their empty honors, and to use the badge that belongs to your rank, so long as they are not sharers in your courage."

Men really do not care how much a woman imitates them sexually. The more she sleeps around, the better they like it. But when she appropriates the *real* perquisites of masculinity they get furious. Honor is a foremost perquisite of masculinity.

One night last winter when I was downtown, it started snowing. It seldom happens in Seattle, but when it does traffic quickly becomes paralyzed because of the steep hills. I live on the steepest. I flagged a cab, but when the driver heard my address he balked and said, "No hills."

"Just drop me at the bottom of the hill, and I'll walk the rest of the way," I said.

"I can't go up no hills on a night like this."

"You don't have to. I wouldn't ride up the hill in this snow, I'd rather walk, it's safer. Just take me to the bottom."

We got to the bottom of the hill, and the driver stopped and looked sheepishly up, up, up at my apartment building.

"You live there, ma'am? Gee, that's awful far to walk in this snow. I'll drive you on up there."

I was already getting out of the cab. "No, a promise is a promise. I said no hills, and I meant it." I paid the fare and gave him a fifteen-percent tip. He drew back as though I had burned him.

"You don't have to give me no tip when I didn't even drive you up the hill!" he exclaimed, horrified.

"I always tip, and we agreed we wouldn't go up the hill," I said. He took the money with reluctance, and I started my trek. He did not drive off immediately, and as I glanced back at him I saw him watching me with an expression of puzzled resentment.

He was mad because I had practiced a male virtue: I made a bargain, and I kept it without whining, manipulating, or changing my mind. *He* was the manipulator; *he* had done the whining, and *he* was the one who changed his mind.

Work—real work, hard work—is another masculine perquisite. Men do not like to see evidence that a woman really works. The messy desk is a case in point. In offices men like to leave their desks in a cyclonic condition, often with little notes to the cleaning staff taped on the lamp that read DO NOT TOUCH! By contrast, there is often a strict rule that secretaries' desks must be completely cleared of everything except the phone at the end of the day. Not a paper in the in-and-out boxes, not a pencil in the tray.

The woman with a messy desk is telling the world that she does something important at that desk.

The woman who is even *in* the office *at* her desk can pose a threat to some men, which is why secretaries and typists can get away with so much absenteeism. The "kindly" boss who does not crack the whip over his flitting, shopping, coffee-drinking female help is not kindly at all; he simply doesn't like to see women working. Now that women are buckling down and working seriously with advancement in mind, a great many men who work with them spend the day in a state of inchoate resentment without fully realizing what it is that bothers them.

I have noticed that men do not mind that I am a writer with several books to my credit. In America, writing is considered vaguely feminine because it is cerebral, indoorsy, and inactive: those who can, do; those who can't, write. Above all, writing is done at home, which makes it "woman's work" to a man's way of thinking. Even being confronted with an actual copy of a woman's book does not threaten men—although they tend to turn it over immediately and look at the photo on the back before paying any attention to its contents. They harbor a curious, rather pretty conviction that books somehow "get written" in odd moments, much the way a Victorian woman eventually finished embroidering a sampler between sickroom vigils when she was nursing her children through diphtheria.

What does bother men is seeing actual evidence of production: two typewriters, a dictaphone, and lots of mess. It is clear to them that something unwomanly and subversive is going on here—like work.

Not really kickable but extremely irritating are men who indulge in certain stock phrases from the male lexicon. Leading the list is: "There's a way you could make better time." Try giving driving directions to someone in front of a man, just try it. He always knows a better way. Does any woman even know where she lives? Of course not. She still writes her address on a piece of paper and pins it to her dress in case she has to ask a nice policeman to help her get home. The role of pathfinder is a male one that men will never let a woman assume. He is also an expert on shortcuts. He will drive around and around looking for the old two-lane back road. He will run out of gas. It does not matter as long as it is a way to make better time.

My mother said she first heard "Let's get out of here" in 1931 during a speakeasy raid. I have heard it in perfectly legal bars, lovely restaurants, and at parties where I was having the time of my life and did not want to leave. The phrase has become a cornerstone of the male's language of seduction; the moment it occurs to him that his date might be interested in going to bed, he will say, "Let's get out of here." Something comes over even the most pleasant, genial man when he says it: he leers, and his eyes turn into George Raft slits as he clamps his lips and speaks out of the side of his mouth. I suspect that it did originate during Prohibition, which is why I like to reply: "Cheese it, the cops!"

Men and telephones are a study in maddening ritualistic behavior. Women regard phones as instruments of convenient communication; men see them as power sticks. "All I have to do is pick up the phone," he brags. All he has to do is call one of his "boys," as Edward G. Robinson would say, to get something "done." After he dials his number, he is mortally offended if he has to wait. "They put me on hold!" he cries, unable to believe it. Women, who have been on hold for centuries, can take such delays with equanimity, but men cannot. Watch a man when he is on hold; he seethes, taps his fingers, grits his teeth, rolls his eyes, and fruitlessly jiggles the buttons on the receiver tray, a signal that has not worked since the days when Central said "Number please."

Few men tending bar in a woman's home fail to utter that incredible question: "Where do you keep your ice?" He assumes that being female, your way of arranging things must be whimsical. Running a close second to this one is the question he asks when the lights go out: "Do you know where your fuse box is?" He is quite willing to play electrician and repair the damage, but no power on earth can make him say, "*Where* is your fuse box?" Third on the list of preposterous inquiries is: "Do you have a shoeshine brush?" Men are convinced that women never clean their shoes—we just keep buying new pairs when the old ones get dirty. Of course I have a shoeshine brush, and saddle soap, too. I also have a bootjack if he needs one.

I am tired of hearing men wax ecstatic over "that quality of vulnerability." A first cousin of this is "that quality of availability" that Kim Stanley had in *The Goddess.* These two phrases are part and parcel of the Marilyn Monroe–Judy Garland cult of recent years. Men would not dare tell a woman that they like these qualities in all females for fear of instigating a feminist diatribe, so they join the Monroe-Garland brigade and couch their male chauvinism in a lot of safe, esoteric talk about star quality, the studio system, and the psychology of the waif.

Men continue to search for these qualities in maddening ways. A favorite means of detecting availability is watching a woman while she reads a sexy novel—or one reputed to be sexy—in a public place. Men on planes and in hotel lobbies stare at a woman reader's face while she is staring at her page. One senses when one is being stared at, so of course the woman looks up, which encourages the man to think that she came to such a sexy passage that she looked up in order to find—him.

They also like to watch a woman's reaction to something horrible or sickening, to see if she will show weakness. In Joan Barthel's book about the Peter Reilly case, *A Death in Canaan,* male reporters and jury members stared at the female jury members while the pathologist showed slides of the murder victim's ravaged body and lacerated vagina. "Edward Ives glanced at Mrs. Wald, sitting beside him in the first row of the jury box.... The reporters, having nothing else to watch, watched the judge and the jury, and mostly the women on the jury."

Men have some vexing gestures and habits that hint at

repressed anger. In supermarkets, they toss items con-
temptuously into their baskets instead of laying them down. At
the checkout counter when the total comes to $20.05, they put
down a twenty-dollar bill and then fish out a nickel and *slap* it
on top of the bill. These things are triggered by a lingering need
to exhibit brusqueness and to make big, cavalier gestures. The
gestures get even bigger and more cavalier when men are
seated next to a woman in a public place. They must invade her
privacy zone, no matter how slightly. They will drape their
elbows over the back of a banquette in a restaurant, and
generally flop, slope, sprawl, or stretch in her direction. It is
never enough to give her reason to complain, but it is there all
the same.

Tufts University president Jean Mayer, who is also a nutri-
tionist, has observed another irritating male habit: "We are the
only country I think of which has male and female foods.
Women eat chicken croquettes, but for the man it's a big slab
of rare meat. It's the motorcycle of the middle-aged, the last
refuge of macho." *

Dr. Mayer neglects to mention the cholesterol fears that have
cut down men's consumption of big slabs of rare meat, but he is
basically right about the psychology of foods. Many men do
not like to see a woman eat a big rare steak. It is just about the
only kind of meat I eat, so I have had plenty of opportunities to
study men's reaction to my carnivorousness. If a man is paying
for my steak, part of him relishes the role of big spender; he is a
man who can afford to feed this trencherperson. But at the same
time, another part of him is a little disturbed. It shows on his
face; men are not good dissemblers. It lasts only a second, but a
certain look flashes and then is gone. We really have not come
very far from the days when Scarlett O'Hara operated on the
theory that men do not like to see women eat.

So, we can't be honorable, we can't work, and we can't eat.
Terrific.

* *Newsweek*, December 19, 1977.

There is nothing quite like three men who try to pick up a lone woman in the hope that she will russle up a couple of girl friends. The first thing they must do is decide which of their number to send over to make the pitch. They huddle, and then one of them gets up and crosses the room. It never fails: they always pick the worst one to represent the group. If *they* were women, they tell themselves, *this* is the kind of guy they would like. He is what men pull out of the hat when they try to practice sexual empathy.

8

LET FLY POYNT BLANCK
or How He Writes

It is an American article of belief that boys make more noise, more mess, and get into more trouble than girls. We believe, furthermore, that this is how it should be. Thanks to this philosophy, we have evolved the male sentence, which makes more noise, more mess, and gets its author into more trouble than sentences written by women.

Let us take as an example the opening sentences of four novels. Many novels open with a description of the weather. It is a good way to begin, for it not only sets the mood of the story, it also serves to answer one of the five essential questions of the journalistic lead: *when.*

Jane Eyre by Charlotte Brontë: "There was no possibility of taking a walk that day."

Valley of the Dolls by Jacqueline Susann: "The temperature hit ninety the day she arrived in New York."

Peyton Place by Grace Metalious: "Indian summer is like a woman."

The Honey Badger by Robert Ruark: "It was that hot—steaming, stinking, sewer-vaporous, New York—humid, solid, soul-smiting hot."

In my most paranoid moments, I have a feeling that male authors often get away with bad writing simply because they are male. A little voice in the editor's unconscious mind says, "Boys will be boys," and the blue pencil, without having writ, moves on through verbal rags and snails, like Ira Levin's compound adjectives. In *The Stepford Wives* we are treated to people who make "I'm-thinking-of-rising movements," a drive past "the you'd-never-guess-what-it-is-from-the-outside non-polluting incinerator plant," and a woman who is not attractive enough to qualify for the category of "once-in-a-lifetime-mustn't-be-missed."

Also not to be missed is the bus in *The Midnight Cowboy*, which makes a rest stop "in Raleigh in North Carolina." James Jones' *Some Came Running* contains a man who experiences a "sexual arouse" for a waitress who refuses to sleep with him because she is an "antifeminist." A jilted lover expresses his heartbreak with a cry containing fifty *h*'s: "Ahhhhhhhhhhhh-hhhhhhhhhhhhhhhhhhhhhhhhhhhhhhhhhhhhhhhhh!" Eight lines later, this same "sentence" is repeated, *h* for *h*. But there is nothing to worry about, according to another Jones character, who advises: "Don't complexify it." Strange advice from an author whose dedication page even needs editing.

Choosing the quintessential James Jones passage is difficult, and copying it is even more difficult, but my favorite is from *The Merry Month of May*.

> But a great phenomenon he had noted (over the years; talking) in a great many American men. They were all of them—or a great, great many; a very high percentage—absolutely cunt-struck. They were almost all, like himself, completely cunt-oriented.... When the true history of his generation came to be written, it might well go down to posterity as the Cunt-Struck Generation. By extension they could then be called Cuntniks....

America is a free country. Everybody's got a right to write

like they want. Nevertheless, I suggest that Jones' passage could have gone something like this.

> In talking to American men over the years he had noted a phenomenon: most of them were as cunt-struck as he. When the history of his generation was written, posterity might well call them the Cunt-Struck Generation, or the Cuntniks.

As a little girl, I was taught to clean up after myself. In the publishing world, cleaning up after oneself is called "polishing" your manuscript. Little boys don't do it. To authors like Jones, polished writing is fraught with psychological peril. Women polish things—our nails, our silver, our manuscripts. A real man writes rough drafts. Neatness, precision, and fussiness are feminine virtues, and searching for *le mot juste* is a sissified pasttime best left to effete European men like Flaubert. "Flaubert me no Flauberts, Bovary me no Bovarys," said Thomas Wolfe when someone suggested that he try to say what he meant in less than 6,000 pages. Length is everything; the longer the better, in books as in other things, and Heaven forbid that anyone should *cut* a male manuscript. "I'd rather be a putter-inner than a taker-outer," said Wolfe.*

The American man's problems with the written word go back three centuries. As Daniel J. Boorstin explains in *The Americans: The Colonial Experience*, the Puritans objected to the elegant, metaphysical Anglican conceits of John Donne and Jeremy Taylor. They sought instead what American men have always sought: virility. John Cotton advised all good men who wished to express their thoughts to "let fly poynt blanck." They took his advice. The sermon became an American institution and our first literature was the spoken rather than the written word. From these beginnings grew sacrosanct male tours de

---

* *The Thirties: A Time to Remember*, Don Congdon, editor.

force such as luncheon speeches, commencement addresses, whistle-stop campaign oratory, filibusters, and unpolished novels.

Men have another writing problem that at first glance seems to be an advantage. "Male writers have always been able to study their craft in university or coffeehouse, group themselves into movements or coteries, search out predecessors for guidance or patronage, collaborate or fight with their contemporaries." *

This is to say, men spend a great deal of time telling each other what they want to hear, and boozing it up in the name of art. Writing, which ought to be synonymous with individualism, becomes, for men, a group grope. The name of the game is to copy the style of the writer who drinks everyone else under the table, or the one who is removed by the police. The novels that result from such imitation invariably are blurbed *slice-of-life, no-holds-barred, searing* and *devastating*. They are usually written in the same voice that the author used on his way to the paddy wagon, that is to say, first-person abrasive, and some have been conceived in what is politely known as a spa.

Masculinity fears cause our writers no end of troubles. Commenting on the terse style of our sacred bull, Ernest Hemingway, critic Leslie Fiedler asked: "What terror drove him to make speech of near-silence we can only guess."

It is not a very hard exercise in guessing. America is the land of strong, silent men. Women talk. Homosexuals chatter. Therefore a real man must say as little as possible. To be laconic is to be masculine. Bite it off. Like this paragraph.

Like Edith Bunker, American men are told to stifle themselves. We all know what happens when Edith tries to remain stifled for too long: more pours out than ever. America's laconic

* Literary Women: The Great Writers by Ellen Moers.

tradition has the same effect on male writers. From time to time, they erupt in a diarrhetic spree of wordiness that might be called *macho hyperbole*.

Take for example the description of female orgasm in the 1963 novel *Stacy Tower*, by Robert H. K. Walter.

> Slowly, powerfully, he moved against her, the very pit of his loins pressing insistently against hers. Without her being aware of the exact instant in which it had begun, a new sensation was stirring in her groin. Until this moment, the sensations, although wonderfully illuminated by a freshness and passion almost forgotten, had been familiar ones. But the new sensation was something strange and unknown. Slowly and quickly it grew—a wild, ominous turbulence; a disturbing, unnameable threat. She experienced an instant of fear, of rising hysteria—TOO MUCH! TOO MUCH!—as when in a dream of dread there is just time to glance back over the shoulder and glimpse the enormous black-green wall of water towering far above one's head, blotting out the sky . . . and then it came crashing down, and she was inundated, washed rapidly away, swept whirling through blind seas of frightful ecstasy; hurled glidingly down dark submarine undercurrents of sensation, at once unbearable and exquisite; spun slowly, weightless, through galactic infinities of delirious tranquility, through lunar orbits of intolerable delight, groaning with pleasure, sobbing with ecstasy, begging, praying, blaspheming. . . .

Ben Ames Williams' misogynistic novels make it clear that he has no use for distaff ways, yet in *Leave Her to Heaven* he lapses into another kind of macho hyperbole in a passage full of girlish fits and starts and parenthetical addenda:

> Her lips looked—he chose the word advisedly, since the choice of words was his delight—delicious, as though if you

bit into them it would be like biting into a sweetmeat, one of those candies which are filled with a pleasant warming liquid. ... He had the feeling—permitting his thoughts to range as they chose—that it would be delightful to nibble at them! ... He remembered the tales in the *Arabian Nights*, heroines with alabaster brows, and almond eyes, and lips—was it lips?—like pomegranates. ... He thought of myrrh and frankincense and potpourri—or was it patchouli?—and of nameless mysterious fragrances. ...

In this passage, Williams sounds exactly like the scatterbrained sorority sister who summarized this story for me: "*Leave Her to Heaven*—he got that from Shakespeare, it says so in the front—is about a woman who drowns her husband's brother because she's so jealous—or is it possessive?—I never can remember the difference. Anyhow, Gene Tierney played her in the movie—she was in *Laura*, too—but they never made a movie out of *The Strange Woman*—or did they?"

The Chandler Heritage by Ben Haas is such a self-consciously masculine novel that one gets the feeling that the real protagonist is not Heath Chandler, but masculinity itself. The word crops up constantly: "Her father ... wooed her carefully back to reality with all the force of his magnetic masculinity." "There was something about the mills wholly, brutally masculine. ..." "Fox was a man in every sense of the word, tolerating no infringement on his masculinity."

Haas has the straightforward style of the natural storyteller and a solid command of language; nonetheless he lapses into a gushy, anthropomorphized love scene in the middle of a test pilot episode.

Then, blessedly, he was alone with the magnificent airplane. It was like making love as its quivering frame responded to his every demand. Climbing, soaring, reaching for the peak of ecstasy, it flung itself against the poised sun in the glittering blue. . . . He pushed it higher, still higher, knowing what it could do and straining for the utmost, just as in the act of sex; and then it reached apogee, trembled in a way that told him it had found fulfillment, could climb no more, and he leveled off. . . . He and the Tiercel were alone up here and making love to one another. . . . He told his darling what he wanted and she responded, hurtling down obediently on her stubby wings, willing to risk self-destruction at his command. . . . The Tiercel whined and shivered and roared with excitement, and he pulled her up and rolled her, and she shook all over with delight and peeled, belly to the sun, back to the sky. He whipped her out, rolled over and over again, weight straining against the belt, mind blurred with an ecstasy of blue sea and sky, dived her down and brought her up once more and sent her soaring. . . . The engine growled and purred with pleasure at the demands he made. . . . Then, at the last minute, he and the plane both were racked as he brought it out; it shuddered with the ferocity of his requirements, but obeyed. . . .

A few lines later, Haas reverts to his usual straightforward style with the terse statement: "And then the engine quit." The next time we meet the *testes* pilot he is in the hospital.

One of the most popular American novels of all time is *Anthony Adverse* by Hervey Allen. I read it when I was eleven, so I could not understand why everybody kept drowning.

The water symbolism in this 1933 novel was appropriated by Hollywood and used for years to suggest sexual culmination. A whole generation of Americans grew up on soggy love scenes. When the waves crashed on the rocks in *From Here to Eternity*, my date turned to me and whispered, "He's in."

The water symbolism in *Anthony Adverse* became such a joke with literary critics that they completely overlooked a much better—and drier—example of macho hyperbole in the 1,224-page tome. Maria Bonnyfeather and Dennis Moore are in the bushes conceiving Anthony. It is perfectly clear what is going on, but Allen could not resist the temptation to gild the lily.

Attracted by so lovely and virginal a store of honey, a bumble-bee lit upon this blossom and after stroking its petals for sometime as if he were in love, began to tear away the small green membrane that still defended it from his assault. The petals opened slightly and began to curl. Settling back as it were upon his haunches, and raking his body back and forth over this small opening, the bee finally succeeded in inserting himself in the flower. Here, as if in ecstasy, he dashed himself about. The flower opening ever wider trembled, and drooped upon its stem.

Much has been said about Hemingway's claim that "the earth moved." Knowing his reputation for terseness, we would expect this line to turn up in a typical bit of Hemingway dialogue. Like this:
"We're together."
"Darling."
"Yes."
"We'll never stop loving each other."
"No."
"The earth moved."
"You're a grand girl."
The famous claim actually comes at the end of a passage that is pure macho hyperbole. As passages go, it leads to nowhere, but there is a lot of it.

For him it was a dark passage which led to nowhere, then to nowhere, then again to nowhere, once again to nowhere, always and forever to nowhere, heavy on the elbows in the earth to nowhere, dark, never any end to nowhere, hung on all time always to unknowing nowhere, this time and again for always to nowhere, now beyond all bearing up, up, up and into nowhere, suddenly, scaldingly, holdingly all nowhere gone and time absolutely still and they were both there, time having stopped and he felt the earth move out and away from under them.

As the anonymous editor advised: "There are two things that cannot be described. One of them is a sunset."

Being embarrassed for someone else is the most painful emotion of all. One need not be a Victorian Gentle Reader to cringe over certain passages in the He genre of American literature. Male omniscience leads inevitably to a babelike innocence and thence to a blind spot that prevents men from realizing what they are putting down on paper.

The most unbearable He prose in *all* literature has to be Herman Melville's short story, "I and My Chimney." When we read it in college, all the girls in the class were either frozen in shame or doubled up with held-in giggles. The boys, on the other hand, did not seem affected by "my chimney—a huge, corpulent old Harry VIII of a chimney—rises full in front of me ... a monster telescope ... it soars from the cellar, right up through each successive floor, till, four feet square, it breaks water from the ridgepole of the roof, like an anvil-headed whale. ..."

When we came to "How my wife's geraniums bud there! Her eggs, too—can't keep them near the chimney on account of hatching," one of the girls moaned, "Oh, honestly!" and we all broke up, to the perplexity of the boys, who still thought this was a story about a chimney.

Sherwood Anderson served up a bushel of cringes in his short story "The Man Who Became a Woman," a classic of unaware latency, but even it cannot compare to a passage in Robert Ruark's novel *The Honey Badger*.

The blurb *devastating* is especially fitting for this novel because it is about a man with cancer of the testicles. Besides being castrated, he must take female hormones, which cause his breasts to grow and his beard to recede. Medical detail is piled upon medical detail, effectively creating a sense of horror that, in gentler hands than Ruark's, could have resulted in true tragedy but for the scene in which the patient asks the doctor for advice about properly fitted trousers.

The doctor replies:

"There are prosthetic devices to replace the testes. I had one case in which I inserted two hollow plastic balls. ... The patient came back and begged me to take them out again. It seems that the membrane which separated them had eroded, and they had a tendency to *click* at the most inopportune moments. We didn't improve his appearance but he was certainly less noisy when he entered the drawing room."

No discussion of He-haw writing would be complete without the works of Erica Jong, winner of the Indira Gandhi Award for Disastrous Imitation.

In *How to Save Your Own Life*, Miss Jong permits herself several careless male freedoms. Like Scott Fitzgerald, she takes the playwright's easy way out rather than bother writing proper dialogue.

ME: Park your car.
HE *(boyish)*: Promise you won't change your mind.
ME *(womanly, reassuring)*: I won't. Silly.

This might appeal to some people as quick 'n' easy reading for our fast-moving era, but it lacks something. To see what it lacks, let us rewrite another female author's dialogue in the same fashion.

HE (*wistfully, very winnowed-out*): She's like me, Scarlett, she's part of my blood and we understand each other.

SHE (*angrily, very Irish*): Why don't you say it, you coward! You'd rather live with that stupid little fool!

HE: You must not say these things about Melanie!

SHE (*very Southern belle-ish*): She's a pale-faced mealy-mouthed ninny and I hate her!

In the end of *How to Save Your Own Life*, where she switches from the first to the third person for no apparent reason, Miss Jong has a field day with macho hyperbole.

The whole world went out except for the throbbing in her cunt, which seemed to her like a universe, a galaxy, a deep black hole in space. . . . It was almost as if the orgasm was not only in her cunt, but in her throat, her voice, her whole body, and the scream was part of it, part of the release. . . . And she thought, feeling that cock slide in and out of her as if it owned her soul, that if she died then, if she died that very minute, it would be all right. . . . They lay not moving in the absolute peace after the *earthquake*. She felt a small sun glowing in her solar plexus, and her legs and arms too heavy to move, mercury-filled moon suits . . . (my italics).

The next time I go to bed with a man, I'm going to take along a jar of Tang.

Miss Jong accepts male fantasies as gospel and uses several phrases beloved by wishful-thinking men: "Her cunt was dripping," "his hot cock," and "feel his spurt." Healthy, responsive women lubricate; when they start dripping they had better get a Pap test before it is too late. An erect penis is not especially hot;

to women, the marblelike smoothness of a full erection rather
suggests coolness. The male's most cherished idée fixe is that a
woman can feel an ejaculation. Every woman has lied to a lover
and said she felt it, simply to please him, but the coarse-grained
vagina is simply not up to such detection. Miss Jong has not yet
made that other beloved male claim, "He felt her spray," but I
shall wait with interest. It is only a matter of time before the
female ejaculation hits the fan.

Miss Jong fails the acid test of female writing as put forth by
H. L. Mencken in *In Defense of Women.*

> The woman novelist, if she be skillful enough to arise out of
> mere imitation into genuine self-expression, never takes her
> heroes quite seriously. From the day of George Sand to the
> day of Selma Lagerlöf, she has always got into her character
> study a touch of superior aloofness, of ill-concealed derision.

Aloofness is not Miss Jong's long suit. Her books are marked
by frantic romanticism. As for her orgasms, having had a few
myself, I strongly suspect that hers arise out of mere imitation.

A good example of how a woman who knows what she's
talking about writes a love scene is found in Edith Wharton's
novel *Ethan Frome.* It is the scene in which Ethan kisses Mattie's
knitting wool.

> . . . a warm current flowed toward him along the strip of stuff
> that still lay unrolled between them. Cautiously he slid his
> hand palm-downward along the table till his finger-tips
> touched the end of the stuff. A faint vibration of her lashes
> seemed to show that she was aware of his gesture, and that it
> had sent a counter-current back to her; and she let her hands
> lie motionless on the other end of the strip. . . . Her glance
> fell on his hand, which now completely covered the end of
> her work and grasped it as if it were a part of herself. He saw

a scarcely perceptible tremor cross her face, and without knowing what he did he stooped his head and kissed the bit of stuff in his hold. As his lips rested on it he felt it glide slowly from beneath them, and saw that Mattie had risen and was silently rolling up her work.

9

PAPER DOLLS
or How He Writes
About Women

"My wife is the reader in the family" is an American maxim. If she reads many He novels, her self-esteem is probably at rock bottom. In He novels, reader identification tends to be a wasting disease that attacks the female pituitary and then spreads.

The voracious sexual gorgon is the He author's favorite character. Her leitmotif is: "Then he saw her." This is one of those laser-beam sentences that signals the reader that something big is coming up. In *The Chandler Heritage* by Ben Haas, something big does come up. Her name is Evelyn Ford, and we meet her as she is getting off work at the cotton mill.

> ... she gave off, without being able to help it, a kind of sexual radiation as palpable as musk, which brought men into rut.... She came toward him ... barefooted, with a slow, indolent gait that caused broad hips to shift and heavy thighs to rub together in lazy invitation beneath the clinging, sweat-moist gingham that culminated higher in a rhythmic bobbing of big, soft, unhaltered breasts. Heath stared at her in helpless fascination, feeling instant stirring in his loins.... Then

she was gone, trailing in her wake like dust setting behind her a diminishing stream of sexuality. . . .

This is the Mighty Thighs genre of He writing, where something is always culminating, where fascinations are always helpless, where invitations are always lazy, where loins are always stirring, and where forgetful earth mothers are forever leaving something in their wake.

It is not necessary to be an adult to be a voracious sexual gorgon. There is also a gorgonette. In *The Strange Woman* by Ben Ames Williams, two-year-old Jenny sits in the lap of the naval officer who has come seeking her mother's sexual favors. To his mixed delight and horror—and helpless fascination—the officer finds himself powerfully aroused and enchanted by this Strange Tot. Needless to say, she grows up to fit the title role.

William Faulkner created a voracious sexual fetus. In *The Hamlet* we meet Eula Varner, "already grown at eight, who apparently had reached and passed puberty in the foetus." Like a foetus, Eula is good at waiting through "accumulating days of burgeoning and unhurryable time" until she is old enough to ruin her first man. She sits "in the same place and almost in the same position, her hands lying motionless for hours on her lap like two separate slumbering bodies."

Eula finally gets around to entering elementary school, where she has a predictable voracious sexual effect. "By merely walking down the aisle between them she would transform the very wooden desks and benches themselves into a grove of Venus and fetch every male in the room. . . ."

She was neither at the head nor the foot of her class . . . because the class she was in ceased to have either head or foot twenty-four hours after she entered it. Within the year there even ceased to be any lower class for her to be promoted from, for the reason that she would never be at either end of anything in which blood ran. It would have but one point, like a swarm of bees, and she would be that point, that center, swarmed over and importuned yet serene and intact and apparently even oblivious, tranquilly abrogating the whole long sum of human thinking and suffering which is called knowledge, education, wisdom, at once supremely unchaste and inviolable: the queen, the matrix.

If we plow through all this atavistic male terror we find that Eula is simply the type that mothers of less yeasty girls call "overdeveloped." Women novelists handle the type much better. In *A Tree Grows in Brooklyn*, Betty Smith views the junior temptress without horror and with considerable comedy.

At ten, Sissy was as fully developed as a woman of thirty, and all the boys were after Sissy and Sissy was after all the boys. At twelve, she started keeping steady company with a lad of twenty. . . . At fourteen, she was going with a fireman of twenty-five . . . this romance ended in the fireman marrying Sissy. . . . She became pregnant a month after marriage. She was still a hoyden girl of fourteen in spite of her womanly status. The neighbors were horrified when they watched her skipping rope on the street with other children, heedless of the yet-to-be-born baby who was now an almost unwieldy bulge. In the hours not devoted to cooking, cleaning, lovemaking, rope skipping and trying to get into the baseball game with the boys, Sissy made plans for the coming baby.

There is a sexpot in every school. Men believe that she is hated by other females. *They* may hate her, but we often feel a kind of warmth for her. The one I remember from high school used purple ink, circled her *i*'s instead of dotting them, and applied makeup while her head was bowed for the Lord's

Prayer. She carried dozens of lipsticks in an enormous cheap plastic kit, and readily offered them to pale honor students with a friendly, "Here, hon, it's your color." She was not stupid. She was justifiably proud of her pretty penmanship and she was very good at math—probably because she sensed she would need it later on. Far from being the scourge of the school, she was practically teacher's pet because she always volunteered for nonacademic tasks like cutting out snowflakes to paste on the windows at Christmas. One weekend she volunteered to take the flag home and wash it. She was a bandbox-neat girl—they are not the slatterns men imagine—so I suppose it was only natural that she starched the flag so stiffly that she had to carry it into class like a sheet of plywood.

If He writers would only relax and regard the sexpot as human, they would realize that there is nobody quite like good old Lilith.

Many of our He writers find it difficult to describe women, so they give up and let their heroines describe themselves. The number of heroines who stand stark naked in front of full-length mirrors mentally intoning, "good tits, good ass, neat dark triangle" is truly amazing. Never mind that women always say *bust* and *behind*; it is not she who is talking, but the He author. Such a woman can be counted on to cup her breasts to see if they are still "firm and perky." They always are because she wouldn't be in the book if they weren't. If she is over thirty-five or has had three or more children, she will search for stretch marks, and if she finds any, she will describe them to herself in masochistic detail—"shiny white striated tracks of fate striping the once rosy-marble flesh of her sweetly curving girl-hips" is a typically He way of putting it. She always rubs her palms down her thighs, like a short-order cook rubbing his greasy hands down his apron when a waitress screams, "Ordering!" She never hurries; like Amelia Barr in *The Honey Badger*, she inspects herself "long and searchingly." Finally she puts her clothes on and leaves the house of mirrors, after a last look around to see if she has left anything in her wake. By this time, she is established in the reader's mind as a shallow, self-absorbed narcissist, whether she actually is or not. Usually she is.

Writers who understand women do not need to resort to a house of mirrors. British author John Fowles introduces Sarah Woodruff, his French lieutenant's woman, as she is staring out to sea, looking at nothing, with a gaze "like a rifle shot." The exquisitely apt phrase establishes her determination and will-power immediately. Another English novel that contains an almost identical scene is Thomas Hardy's *The Return of the Native*, in which we meet the unforgettable Wessex Juno, Eustacia Vye, as she stands alone on a bleak heath, gazing out over the landscape with that most masculine of looking glasses, a telescope. Ivan Turgenev picked the most difficult technique of all when he described Elena in *On the Eve*. We meet her while she is gazing out the window in a reverie, an activity entirely different from looking into a mirror. Elena is looking *away* from her physical self and into the puzzle of her own personality, trying to figure out what it is that makes her different from all the other nice Russian girls.

Comparing women to dangerous animals is another favorite descriptive dodge of our He authors. Not surprisingly, game hunter and safari veteran Robert Ruark has bagged us most memorably in a passage that was used as a blurb on his book jacket.

There is a bloody brave little animal in Africa called the honey badger. It may be the meanest animal in the world. It kills for malice and for sport, and it does not go for the jugular—it goes straight for the groin. It has a lot in common with the modern American woman.

Shrikes, shrews, black widow spiders, praying mantises, the list is endless. Anything that hisses or gobbles will do. The He writer cannot describe the feral quality of the female without dehumanizing her, but it can be done. Thomas Hardy did it in *Tess of the D'Urbervilles* in a way that suggests the mawlike aspect of the open vulva without once venturing below the chin.

> She was yawning, and he saw the red interior of her mouth as if it had been a snake's. She had stretched one arm so high above her coiled-up cable of hair that he could see its satiny delicacy above the sunburn; her face was flushed with sleep, and her eyelids hung heavy over their pupils. The brimfulness of her nature breathed from her.

Many critics have said that James Jones could not write believable women. The Big He could not write believable respectable women, but no one had a surer touch with tramps.

In *Some Came Running*, Ginnie Moorehead, who works at the brassiere factory in C cup, is "the biggest free romp in Parkman, Illinois." When the hero of the novel, Dave Hirsh, asks his buddy, 'Bama Dillert, to get him a woman—the Jonesian phrase for a blind date—Ginnie turns up as one of the candidates. 'Bama explains that while Ginnie loves sex and is the easiest made woman of the group, "she looks horrible, looks like a regular pig." 'Bama, who is anything but sexually fastidious (he beds a woman known as the Terre Haute Wreck), has slept with Ginnie only once. He couldn't take any more.

Dave finds Ginnie repulsive, but he does not feel like making the effort to seduce any of the harder-to-get candidates, so he picks Ginnie. They go to his room and have four "romps." It is during one of these that Jones begins deftly to characterize Ginnie in a way that lifts her out of the common barfly category and into the realm of egomania.

> Ginnie did something which startled him half to death. Staring wildly and almost blindly at the ceiling, she cried out

to herself in a loud, penetrating voice: "Oh, Ginnie, Ginnie, Ginnie!" ... almost as if he were not even there. He was powerless to understand it, or what she meant by it. Nobody with as little ... self-insight as Ginnie could be a bona-fide narcissist, could they?

Dave's naive belief that such a lumpish, stupid woman could not possible be dangerous establishes the chilling theme of the novel in one brushstroke. Jones constantly juxtaposes Ginnie's lethargy with the meanness in her soul. Her dullness is emphasized, so that the word becomes her leitmotif. She moves with the heavy tread of the slattern, yet she has "the sort of held-in quality of a distrustful and watchful animal ... a sort of waspish, irascible, nervous hawklike quality that showed nowhere except in a tiny brilliant pinpoint in the very deepest bottom of the dull eyes. ..."

Ginnie horrors follow Ginnie horrors. She has some engaging habits. "I don't like to see you picking your goddamned nose when I'm getting ready to take you home and go to bed with you!" Dave shouts at her. In an incredible scene, she buys nine copies of Dave's novel and autographs them for her co-workers at the brassiere factory. To her way of thinking, she has a right to do it because by now she is Dave's steady girl.

Dave chides her for appropriating his author's privilege. "Of all the damned ignorant dumb stupid sons of bitches in the whole damned world that I ever heard of, you take the cake. A fat pig of a one-nighter. ... Autographing *stories!* The biggest, fattest, dumbest, laziest, most useless, most worthless most ignorant most *stupid* whore in Parkman!"

In a weak moment when his life has fallen apart, Dave remembers the old army saying that whores make the best wives because they're grateful, and decides to marry Ginnie. The story of their marriage is almost unbearable; Jones brings the reader to the edge of hysteria with his flawless understanding of the psychology of the reformed trollop. As soon as

Ginnie becomes a respectable married woman, she changes completely. She turns frigid because it's not ladylike to enjoy sex. She drops her brassiere-factory girl friends because they're too low-class, and starts going to the Church of Christ. Soon she is ashamed of its evangelical fervor and sets her sights on the Methodist church. Formerly an imbiber of straight rye with a beer chaser, she switches to more refined cocktails. She permits Dave and herself two, no more, before dinner, and they must be drunk out of the proper kind of glass. She collects green stamps and redeems them for copper-bottom pans which she keeps polished and hung on the kitchen wall. Her home is spotless; she becomes the most house-proud woman in town. She even starts a ragbag.

Dave's brother Frank, whom he detests, is a member of the country club. Ginnie decides that she wants to join the country club, too, and nags Dave to patch up his quarrel with his brother. Next she nags him to go into business with his brother and get rich. The final irony occurs when Dave is murdered by one of Ginnie's former lovers and she inherits his share of the business that he started with Frank. Now status-obsessed Frank finds that his partner is status-obsessed Mrs. Virginia Moorehead Hirsh, née the biggest free romp in Parkman, Illinois.

Ginnie lacks even one redeeming quality, yet not only do we believe her, we can never really dislike her. One neither likes nor dislikes a laboratory experiment. Jones' consummate knowledge of sluts leads the reader into a detached, Zola-like interest in cause and effect. If the Ginnie sections of this novel were lifted out and made into a separate, shorter book, it would rank with *Nana, Thérèse Racquin,* and *McTeague.*

Jones' troubles begin when he tries to characterize Ginnie's polar opposite, Gwen French. In Jones country, it's all right to characterize a bad girl but you mustn't lay a pen on a good girl. He seems to realize that he has not done a very good job on Gwen because in his author's note he tells us: "There is a character in this novel which may cause surprise, or consternation, or even disbelief, among certain types of readers: that of the lady school teacher."

Note the *which*. As soon as Jones even *mentions* a decent woman his grammar starts to fall apart.

Gwen French is a thirty-five-year-old virgin whose only sexual outlet is looking at her father's pornography collection and beaming color slides of naked women into the darkened streets outside their home. Gwen's leitmotif is "bull-throated laugh." Sometimes Jones calls it "a very unladylike roar of laughter" or "a healthy indelicate roar of laughter." It is his way of telling us—and himself—that nice girls are human, too, but it doesn't work. The reader soon starts to visualize Gwen leading the stampede in *Elephant Walk*.

For the most part, Jones' style in the Ginnie sections is excellent, but the moment he places Dave in a scene with Gwen, his style goes to pot. While Gwen is cooking dinner, Dave, overwhelmed by a romantic longing for her, compares himself to the ill-starred François Villon in a passage that sounds positively psychotic.

> Poor Villon, he thought, poor François the conny-catcher, the doddipol Gnat-Snatcher, in his Paris squalor, and his fear of the Patrol, and the gibbet of Montfaucon always touching him lightly on the shoulder—what he wouldn't have given to be here. Him and his insane disease of love, love, love, and his Katherine de Vausselles.

That's what a nice girl does to an old army man.

Dave propositions Gwen but she turns him down. She is afraid that if she sleeps with him, he will "find out" that she is still a virgin and laugh at her. We must accept this bizarre reasoning because Jones asks us to. If Gwen's intact hymen is the only thing keeping her from having an affair with Dave, why doesn't she destroy it with her finger instead of agonizing for 1,266 pages? Jones does not raise this question because he has something even more bizarre in store for us.

Dave and Gwen have a highly charged platonic relationship for four years. When he is murdered, she is so full of remorse that she decides to offer him her hymen as a posthumous gift. She has it surgically removed by a gynecologist in Indianapolis, telling herself: "It would not only be a penance. It would, she felt, in some way, also be a redemption." This sentence comes too soon after Ginnie's green stamps not to bring forth a bull-throated laugh from the reader.

On the last page of the novel, Gwen thinks about the operation she has just undergone. "It really had been nothing. One small sharp pain, and that was all. Such a simple thing. Just nothing. Just practically nothing at all. Well, she was what she was now, at least, at any rate."

Well, at any rate, the woman reader can identify with Ginnie, at least. Just one small sharp pain, and then you, too, can be the biggest free romp in Parkman, Illinois.

There is nothing worse than being caught in a Boy Book. It is easy to do because He writers love Boy Books. Leslie Fiedler believes that of all American writers, "only Henry James completely escapes classification as a writer of juvenile classics."

Some He writers are sunk in outright boy-worship, especially of boys around thirteen. It is not surprising that boys of this age should appeal to American men. Thirteen combines the best of two male worlds. It is the age of perpetual erection, yet it is close enough to childhood to embody the joyous exuberance of male purity—i.e., Adam with a full set of ribs.

The Puerulus Prize surely goes to Ben Ames Williams, who created the most cloying little boy in popular fiction: Danny, the crippled kid brother in *Leave Her to Heaven*. We know from the title alone that this is a story about an evil woman. We do not have to read very far to know that a little boy is going to play Mazda to her Ahriman.

The female protagonist—but most certainly no heroine—is Ellen Berent, that monster of possessiveness who marries lantern-jawed Richard Harland solely because he looks like her late father, whom she also possessed. After Richard and Ellen return from their honeymoon, they go to the polio sanitarium to pick up Danny, who is going to live with them. Danny's leitmotif is "clear, happy, boyish tones." As he waits for his big brother's arrival, he is as breathless as a debutante because Richard is his best beau.

> Danny was so merry all that day that the nurses teased him about his love for Dick, declared he was as excited as a girl waiting for her sweetheart; but Danny laughed at their teasing, enjoying it. . . . He lay awake that night, unable to sleep, counting to himself every turn of the wheels which brought Dick nearer and nearer. . . . Then Dick bent over him, saying huskily, "Hi, Danny!" and leaning down to kiss him; and Danny flung his arms around Dick's neck and hugged him tight, and they were both laughing with tears in their eyes, Danny's small body straining up to Dick's; and oh, but Dick felt good in his arms!

Ellen, Richard, and Danny go to the family retreat in the North Woods of Maine. The summer wears on, with Danny constantly in the way of the newlyweds. One day he announces that he is now strong enough to swim across the lake, if only he had someone to accompany him in a rowboat, just in case. "I'll help you," says Ellen. Cut to Gene Tierney sitting motionless in the boat, exquisite cheekbones like falcon's wings in her expressionless face as she waits for Danny to sink for the third time.

Now Ellen has Richard all to herself again. She becomes

pregnant, but that is easily taken care of. She throws herself down the stairs in her sixth month, providing Williams with a line that is a masterpiece of contradiction: "The baby, a lusty boy, was dead." Male infants in He novels are frequently called "lusty."

In a final burst of evilness, Ellen spoils the fun at a rustic macho picnic by poisoning herself in the middle of it, leaving behind enough trumped-up evidence to pin the blame on Richard. He is tried and acquitted of her murder and finds true love with Ellen's gentle, self-effacing sister Ruth. Now he is truly happy again. He has Danny back in a way, because Ruth talks like the Boy Scout Manual: "I don't think it's what you get out of church, it's what you take into it. ... The world is so darned full of nice, ordinary people, Dick, doing their daily jobs. They may be tricky or cruel or something during the week, but they turn to church on Sunday."

Every woman with whom I have ever discussed this novel has said: "Didn't you just *love* Ellen?" and "Ugh! That kid!"

Into every book a little sunshine must fall, else editors start to fret about something called "balance."

I have some favorite He authors. Number one on my list is James M. Cain. He understands women, *likes* women, and can characterize a roaring bitch without getting emotionally involved.

Thanks to Ann Blythe, everyone knows Mildred Pierce's daughter, Veda, but the best scene in the novel was left out of the movie. For purposes of plot simplification, the film Veda became a cabaret singer, but in the book she was a coloratura soprano who took the opera world by storm. It is through this situation that we met Mr. Treviso, her voice teacher, whose blunt appraisal of his pupil's character first opens Mildred's eyes. At no point in the whole novel does Cain intrude to express *his own* opinion of Veda. He lets Mr. Treviso do it with his hilarious broken English and his resigned continental realism.

Mildred bristles with outraged mother love when Mr. Treviso compares Veda to a snake. "Are you insinuating that my daughter is a snake?" she snaps, and Mr. Treviso shrugs and replies:

No—is coloratura soprano, is much worse. All a coloratura always take, never give, all act like duchess. All borrow ten t'ousand buck, go to Italy, study voice, never pay back a money. Marry a banker, get a money, kick out a banker, marry a baron, get da title. 'Ave a sweetie on a side, guy she like to sleep wit'. Den all travel together, all over Europe—a baron, 'e travel in Compartment C, take care of dog. A banker, 'e travel in Compartment B, take care of luggage. A sweetie, 'e travel in Drawing Room A, take care of coloratura.... Da girl is lousy. I tell you, is snake, is bitch, is coloratura.

Cain never shied away from any aspect of female psychology. His novel *Galatea* concerns a monstrously fat woman who falls in love with the ex-fight trainer who puts her on a diet. This is a woman who would never stand in front of a mirror. The book opens with her fall into a muddy ditch. She is too fat to climb out, and is wallowing, literally, in the hole when the drifter-hero comes along and sees her. He raises her with ropes. To show her gratitude, she persuades her husband to give him a job as handyman on the place. The hero, who knows how to get weight off boxers, slims her down to a sylph, infuriating her husband, whose security lies in her repulsiveness. Now that she is thin, the plot is thick with conflict and suspense. Cain handles this difficult theme so deftly and naturally that the woman reader identifies with the heroine even when she looks her worst.

An author very much like Cain is Ludwig Lewisohn. His novel *The Tyranny of Sex* was banned when it was first published in 1927 because of its indictment of marriage, American sexual mores, and its loathsome wife-and-mother protagonist, Anne Vilas, whose thanatophidian ethics would make the novel unbearable to read were it not for Lewisohn's utter objectivity. In the hands of a lesser artist, Anne would be too grotesque to be believable, yet we not only believe her, we grow physically *afraid* of her as we read Lewisohn's emotionless account of her coarseness and brutality. Yet at no point does *The Tyranny of Sex* become misogynistic; even the masculine preference for young women is expressed in a purely objective way, and the passage evokes a cello chord of recognition in the reader's vitals: "When she leaned her cheek against an embroidered pillow . . . the pattern of the heavy thread remained for minutes upon a cheek that had long lost the tautness and resilience of youth."

Like Cain, Lewisohn does not scatter his shot. Anne, like Veda, is not *all* women; she is simply herself, one woman, one bitch. Her viciousness has nothing to do with her sex. Rather, she, her two daughters, and her son all have the same tragic flaw in their natures. *The Tyranny of Sex* is actually an examination of Original Sin in its concrete manifestations as opposed to the abstractions of theologians.

Female narcissists are a dime a dozen in He novels but the true female egomaniac is rare, thanks to the widespread male conviction that women do not have egos. Sinclair Lewis corrected that misconception with his portrayal of the evangelist, Sister Sharon Falconer in *Elmer Gantry*. She so dominates the book that after her death in the fire early on, there *is* no book—a fact that Richard Brooks noted when he ended his movie version with the fire.

Sharon is magnificently insane. Most He writers descend to the ludicrous when characterizing a madwoman. Usually they blame her problems on sexual frustration or the menopause, but Lewis avoided these traps in his creation of Sharon. Born Katie Jonas on the wrong side of the tracks, she changed her name to something she felt suited her hawklike personality. When Elmer asks her if she loves him, she replies airily: "Oh, yes. A little. I'm as fond of you as I can be of anyone except Katie Jonas."

Sharon is monstrous at times, but Lewis never allows her to become a monster. He also lets her express the fully panoply of female moods. He draws her as a chameleon, but she is never allowed to be merely flighty. Most men do not know the difference, but Lewis obviously does:

It was Sharon who was incalculable. Sometimes she was a priestess and a looming disaster, sometimes she was intimidating in a grasping passion, sometimes she was thin and writhing and anguished with chagrined doubt of herself, sometimes she was pale and nunlike and still, sometimes she was a chilly business woman, and sometimes she was a little girl. In the last, quite submissive role, Elmer loved her fondly—except when she assumed it just as she was due to go out and hypnotize three thousand people.

All women would like to be chameleons in the Sharon manner but so few men will permit it. Lewis does permit it, and even revels in it. It is his evident understanding and acceptance of female complexity that makes *Elmer Gantry*, at least in the Sharon section, such an oddly comforting novel.

American men prefer spring chicken. This is a fact that needs no footnoting. This situation has resulted in a great deal of heartbreak and a great many jail sentences, but it has had one good effect: He authors often manage to create good older-woman figures. The reason for their success is not hard to find.

The woman who is no longer desirable is, in effect, no longer a woman. Her invitations have stopped being lazy and have become extremely brisk and businesslike, and, wonder of wonders, there is not a thing trailing in her wake.

Faulkner's older women are superb, and so are Steinbeck's Ma Joad and the coach's wife in Larry McMurtry's novel *The Last Picture Show*. The list is endless, but my favorite creator of older women is James Leo Herlihy. There are certain passages in *The Midnight Cowboy* about Joe Buck's haphazard grandmother that are heartbreakingly tender. Sally Buck had "knees that made you cry they were so sorry-looking and knobby. If there is some part of every loved one that will make you cry to contemplate it, such for Joe were these poor, sad, bony knees of Sally Buck."

Herlihy achieves an olfactory sense in another passage that evokes the funny, sad, ingratiating *Djer Kiss* and *Ben-Gay* smell of old women.

> Sally Buck. He couldn't remember why he'd ever loved her so much: silly, pinch-faced old chatterbox, never sat still, always dabbing at her nose with perfume so you couldn't smell the liquor (but you could anyway), or pulling dollar bills out of her pocketbook to buy off old promises she'd made, forever fooling with a compact or picking lint off her dress whenever you tried to tell something to her. All he could think of in her favor was how spindly her legs were and how sad it was to look at her big bony knees when she crossed them.

In *All Fall Down*, Herlihy achieves the impossible: a convincing girl-talk scene. Annabel Williams and her visitor, Echo O'Brien, are having coffee in the kitchen when Annabel brings up the subject of her advancing age.

Listen, Echo. . . . Less than a year ago, our Dr. Bolz looked me over. Nothing serious, I had some kind of a boomp-boomp-boomp in the heart, *you* know, not a thing but nerves. Anyway, he said that just looking at my body, I could be way, way, *way* under forty. . . . I am not a vain person, but let me tell you, that did wonders for my morale. Now, this is a terrible thing to call attention to, but you know when a woman gets older, how her nipples turn a kind of brown?— Well, mine are still pink. *Pink!*

Only the most apoplectic radical feminist would consider this scene insulting. To any woman who has ever had a girl-talk, it rings so true you can almost smell the coffee.

10

THE BOOK OF
LAMENTATIONS
or These Are My Jewels

When a woman of fashion asked Cornelia, the mother of the
Gracchi, to show her her jewels, the worthy Roman matron put
her arms around her children and said, "These are my jewels."

Here are mine.

The Perpetual Preppie is named Tony. He is the kind of
Tony who is a crew man rather than a hit man because he is
always a Wasp. Unfortunately, he now wears his hair long—
unfortunate because there is nothing quite like a gray crew cut.

In the 1956 St. Swithin's yearbook, which he still keeps on
his coffee table, Tony is described as "a man who is always in a
hurry, but who always has time for his friends." This is
chaplain talk for somebody who does six things at once and
none of them right. Most Wasps are not extroverts, but those
who are seem to feel that they have to atone for the rest of us.
Tony put on *The Trojan Women*, designed the sets, sewed the
costumes, built the cardboard walls of Ilium, wrote the ads,
painted the posters, sold the tickets, and played Andromeda.

Tony managed to maintain a C-plus average at St. Swithin's
thanks to his ingenious cribbing methods, like writing algebraic
equations on his penis and then asking for permission to go to

the bathroom during exams. All sorts of useful information could be found on Tony's penis. Once in the library, when somebody wanted to know when was the Battle of Waterloo, Tony unzipped his fly, whipped it out, and said, "1815." It saved a trip to the encyclopedia.

Tony's conversation revolves around fond memories of boyish pranks. "I'll never forget the time" is his standard opener. What follows are mice in the chapel, Ex-Lax in the brownies, cellophane over the toilet seat, the dog in heat at the headmaster's garden party, explosions in the chem lab, and the time Poot Farrar made an unfortunate noise during the Prize Day speech, hence his nickname.

Every Tony has a Poot Farrar, because every St. Swithin's has one. Poot was the hero of the school, "the greatest all-round athlete we ever had." Tony worships Poot. When he shows you his graduation picture and you ask him where he is, he always says: "I'm standing next to Poot Farrar." This is how old St. Swithin's boys measure renown. If Poot Farrar appeared on the Vatican balcony with the Pope, they would say, "Look who's standing next to Poot Farrar."

I heard so much about Poot that I asked Tony if I could meet him. Slowly he shook his head, his eyes misting.

"He's a vegetable," he said in a broken voice. "He's in a wheelchair, paralyzed from the neck down."

"Was he hurt in a football game?" I asked innocently.

"No, it happened after the Founders' Day banquet. We were horsing around and. . . ."

I had visions of Harold Lloyd hanging on the minute hand of the clock. It seems that Poot made a bet with the other old boys that he could stand on top of a car going eighty miles an hour. He lost.

Life is one big long prank to Tony, and he counts time by semesters. To him, September is the first month of the year. Next to Poot Farrar, he talks most about his old headmaster, and like the boys in *The Rector of Justin,* Louis Auchincloss' novel about an Endicott Peabody figure, he never stops writing long, childish letters to him. These "tear-drenched tributes" are yet another indication that "in respect to Dr. Prescott most of his graduates had never grown up. They continued to love him or hate him as if they were still at school and to praise or excoriate him as if they were in a bull session in the cellar or a canoe on the Lawrence River."

Tony would rather drink than do anything. "Let's get *stinking!*" is his favorite invitation. His drinking is the kind that goes on for days with no food except a few prairie oysters to prevent dry heaves. New York Tonys wake up in San Francisco and vice versa, with no idea how they got there. Typical Tony phone calls open with, "What day is it?" and "Would you come and get me, I lost my shoes at the Red Grotto." He's always calling from pay phones in places with names like the Chinese Gypsy or the Basque Beret.

One night I booked a roomette on the Pullman from Raleigh to New York and Tony escorted me to the train. I had never ridden in a Pullman before, so Tony came into the roomette with me to show me how the bed works. He fiddled with the mechanism, and suddenly the bed popped out and came down, pinning him against the wall. I tried to get it back up but it wouldn't budge. I went to find a porter but they had all vanished. I returned to the roomette and the train started to move. Tony started to laugh. The train moved faster, and he laughed harder. He took a flask from his pocket, swigged, and laughed some more. "This'll make a great story for next Founders' Day!" Then and there, he started rehearsing the story, polishing it here, punching it up there, while I clawed at the bed to no avail. He rode all the way to Wake Forest before I could find a porter to get him loose. Wake Forest is the most Baptist of towns, but Tonys always know where to find "a man with a dog," as they put it. He got hold of a fifth, drank it all, and didn't show up at work for three days. Afterward he referred to this contretemps as "one of the greatest nights of my life."

It's the only kind of great night you can have with Tony. The tongue in the ear is his favorite form of eroticism. He is also a nuzzler of necks, which he accompanies with bearish sounds like "grrrr" and "wruf," but matters tend to stay at this playful level. It's just as well because I really would not want to sleep with Tony. I'd be afraid he would tickle my feet, or that I would find a frog in the bed or *Post No Bills* written on his penis.

I grew up with a father who could fix anything. He converted a candle-holding chandelier to electricity and built new cabinets for the kitchen. The car never saw the inside of a garage because he knew how to do all the things that cars need done to them. If anything went wrong when he was away, Granny summoned "the men." Emma would say something like, "Miss Lura, dis sink stopped up. We got to git de mens in here." Afterward, we said, "The men came today." On a word association test, I would say *men* if the psychiatrist said *fix*.

Then I met Sidney Lowenstein.

In *David Meyer Is a Mother*, Gail Parent wrote that Jewish men can barely turn on their television sets. In *The Status Seekers*, Vance Packard said that they do not have the temperament for puttering. Sidney did change a washer once but he forgot to turn the water off first. Otherwise his attitude toward do-it-yourself was, "I don't know, you could get killed that way." Whenever a chain-saw commercial came on, he would say, "I don't know, they shouldn't sell those things." He was afraid of injuring himself and he was convinced that the injured part would "swell up, turn black, and fall off." This was the watchword of his childhood.

Sidney would not eat bacon, not because he was Orthodox but because he was afraid the grease would ignite while he was cooking. When the home fire extinguisher commercial came on, he would say, "See? It could happen to anybody." He bought one of the fire extinguishers and put it on his kitchen wall. He had to get the janitor to put it up for him. He never believed that a locked door was really locked, so whenever he left his apartment he would stand in the hall twisting his doorknob until his neighbors thought he was trying to break in. "I like to be sure," he said. He finally managed to break the doorknob.

He was horrified by my habit of fixing myself instead of going to doctors. "Never put anything in your ear except your elbow," he warned. "You could go deaf that way." When I picked out a splinter with a needle sterilized in bourbon he predicted gangrene. He mixed excellent martinis but he refused to spear the olives with toothpicks. "Listen, a toothpick can kill you. That's what happened to Sherwood Anderson. He was eating hors d'oeuvres and swallowed just a tiny sliver of a toothpick and he got peritonitis." He snapped his fingers. "Dead!"

Yet despite his obsession with peril, he did something I would never do: he gambled. I have never had the slightest urge to place a bet on anything. I have lived in the Far West for six years but I have never been to Las Vegas. No one in my family gambled; we didn't even play cards for pleasure. I asked Sidney why he enjoyed gambling and he said, "I don't know, the risk I guess." A lot of Jewish men are gamblers; like the James Caan character in the movie *The Gambler*, the risk has a masochistic appeal for them because it re-creates the danger and tensions of living in a Gentile world.

I finally fixed Sidney. I cut an ad out of a men's magazine and taped it to his fire extinguisher. It read: *Here it is, shark-hunters, what you've been waiting for! The Jaws Charter! 6 days in the infested waters of the Great Coral Reef!*

I have never been involved with a creep, but I am aware of them as never before. All women are. Because magazines like

Penthouse will print anything under the sun, today's women are exposed to the kind of men we only heard about in the past. Our mothers told us about poor unfortunate men who couldn't help themselves, but we never really believed they existed because they stayed in the woodwork.

Now they have broken into print all over the place. Women can pick up a magazine and meet, for example, the Prissy Fiend. His letters are marked by a tone of cloying pseudogentility; he substitutes *purchase* for *buy*, *assist* for *help*, and *sufficient* for *enough*. Instead of writing, "I met a sexy girl," the Prissy Fiend writes, "I made the acquaintance of a most attractive young lady." It seems she offered him her dildo, so "I had the pleasure of inserting it in her exceedingly oleaginous Mountain of Venus." Thanks to pornography in general and reader mail in particular, every maniac in near-illiterate America knows how to spell *lubricious* and *oleaginous*.

The Prissy Fiend tends to be a bondage freak, probably because it, too, suggests gentility: S-M has been a gentleman's aberration ever since Algernon Swinburne extolled the Eton whipping post. The Prissy Fiend writes: "Having ample means from an inheritance, several wills, and trust funds, not to mention money that was left to me [?], I have a large and well-kept supply of bondage equipment, including restraining belts an inch and three-quarters wide, made of excellent quality morocco leather, lined with peau de soie. Two straps, approximately fourteen inches long, were stitched together back to back diagonally about six inches from the buckle ends. . . ."

Letters like this ramble on forever with the most picky exactitude. Those that tell how to shave pubic hair in geometric patterns are even worse—the hypotenuse of the clitoris, don'tcha know? This sort of thing does not make women dream of exotic sexual experiences. It reminds me of the times I had to read Granny's knitting instructions aloud to her when she had misplaced her glasses. The Prissy Fiend and all of the Name Withheld fruitcakes who take penis in hand only serve to give all men a bad name. Women now look at men with a jaundiced eye. Is the nice lawyer at the dinner party really a letters-to-panthouse boy? Worse, are *all* men nuts?

The epistolary phase of the sexual revolution is particularly nerve-wracking to any woman who has worked on a newspaper, as I have, and seen what regular contributors to the letters column are often like. They are rattlesnake handlers. Angry, frustrated people are always compulsive letter writers, and their letters have one chilling thing in common: they never change their typewriter ribbons, so that the *o* key penetrates the ribbon entirely and leaves what look like bullet holes.

The Prissy Fiend reminds me of the kind of women who swap household hints in newspaper columns. A Prissy Fiend letter-to-the-editor that I cherish states: "I always clean under my foreskin thoroughly and dust the area with talcum or cornstarch in hot weather." I was going to send this to Heloise, but she died.

Any woman who goes in for higher education, unless she goes to Bob Jones University, is bound to tangle sexually with a professor.

Life in the groin of academe is never simple. Instead of making the pitch like an ordinary man, the professor must try to seduce a girl by giving her a special assignment. This is his way of getting her into his office.

Thanks to this habit, I had to plough through Henry George's treatise on the single tax. When I entered the professor's office, he emerged from behind a huge pile of papers and books on his desk and gave me a glittering smile. As his pipe punctuated his sentences with *puck-puck* he mumbled the professorial version of the sweet nothing.

"Special assignment for you . . . couldn't give it to any of the other students . . . not your caliber . . . *puck-puck* . . . it's an oral report . . . just your cup of tea . . . *puck-puck* . . . requires a little supplementary reading."

I had thought that the War of Jenkins' Ear was crazy-making, but it couldn't compare to the single tax. It was the most ghastly subject I ever tackled. I don't know how I managed to make my oral report, and I don't remember what I said, but somehow I got through it. When I went to the professor's office to return the book, he gave me another glittering smile.

"Excellent report . . . solid grasp of the material . . . most unusual . . . nobody understands Henry George as a rule . . . *puck-puck* . . . *Progress and Poverty* is one of the few really great books . . . *puck-puck* . . . I like his theory of cartels . . . *puck-puck* . . . you ever had a dick in your mouth?"

The man in the local television commercial is a cross to bear. He is constantly jolting women out of lush reveries. Recently I was indulging in the American woman's standard late-night activity: watching *Wuthering Heights.* Merle Oberon clasped her hands and cried out in ecstasy, "Heathcliff! Fill my arms with heather!"

Suddenly everything went color. On the screen appeared a man in a red blazer with a company logo on his breast pocket. He wore a bow tie and a simpleminded grin. His ears wiggled as he spoke.

"Hi! I'm Len Willikins of Beat-Em-All Appliances. We are your friendly dealers. In the best of kitchen appliances. We are having a sale. We want you to come. To our mid-year jamboree. On Route 117. We have lots of late-model. Stoves. Remember our slogan. We beat 'em. All. So come on. Out. Thank. You."

Len Willikins is always on late at night when the most romantic movies are shown. Myrna Loy welcomes Fredric March back from the war with the most lambent look that ever crossed a female face, and then *bang!* There's Len Willikins with a pitch for the Last Chance Business School. Helen Hayes dies in Gary Cooper's arms—followed by Len Willikins for the Et Tu Brute Loan Company. The only time Len Willikins' appearance is satisfying is just after Paul Muni points his finger and says, "I accuse!"

According to the Pollyannas of the sexual revolution, women my age should have affairs with young men. Erica Jong definitely thinks so. In *How to Save Your Own Life* her heroine extols the "puppyish exuberance" of her young man, whose penis reminds her of all-day suckers and candy canes, and whose "sneakers were dirty and, touchingly, had torn laces. The laces on one (the right) were undone."

How sweet. Perhaps he felt that Tugboat Annie would not expect him to dress up. In any case, she can have him because to me there is no one more wearying than a Cockerel of the Walk.

First of all, there's his nostalgia freak-out. He talks constantly about old movies and needs no encouragement whatsoever to recite whole passages of dialogue from them. His bright-eyed, bushy-tailed enthusiasm is exhausting. "Do you remember when Lauren Bacall said, 'You know how to whistle, don't you? Just put your lips together and blow.' Like I mean, wasn't it great?"

Yes, son, I remember it. I saw it the first time it came out. I also remember the giant squid in *Reap the Wild Wind*, so kindly refrain from doing an imitation of it. Nor do I care which Tarleton twin had the first line in *Gone With the Wind*. Yes, I know it was Brent, who was played by Fred Crane, and that the names got mixed up in the credits, so that George Reeves was listed as Brent although he really played Stuart. And yes, I also know that George Reeves played Superman. *But I don't care!*

The Cockerel also wants the older woman to tell him stories. His favorite story, which I am qualified to tell, is The Day Roosevelt Died. "It was unusually hot for April. The radio was on and I was listening to Tom Mix when suddenly John Daly's voice interrupted. . . ." The Cockerel cannot get enough of this sort of thing. He probes for the smallest detail. The reason for his interest is obvious. He is the product of an unheroic age and he longs for leaders whom he can worship. To him, a woman who remembers Roosevelt is like someone who has seen the face of God, and he uses her as a pipeline to the kind of world he craves.

He is without direction, like a bottle with a note in it that the shipwreck victim tosses out to sea. It is this inchoateness, this lack of inner resources that make him hard to take. Anna Karenina's Count Vronsky, for all his youthful faults, lived by a set of unbreakable rules. His code might have been silly but it was *his*: he paid his gambling debts immediately but he let his tailor wait. The Cockerel lets everybody wait while he searches for what he calls "the real me." It is a treasure hunt from which I prefer to be excused.

Whatever the Cockerel majors in, his eternal stumbling block is *relevancy*. He knows all there is to know about the United Nations, but he has no idea what the Entente Cordiale was. He follows Begin and Sadat so closely that he even knows when they go to the bathroom, but he does not know who Esther, Mordecai, and Haman were—even if he is Jewish. He can hold forth for days on Henry Kissinger, but Warwick the Kingmaker rings no bells in his "now"—obsessed brain. William "Bill" Fletcher's time capsule is labeled "1940" but the Cockerel's is labeled "11:15 this morning."

He is a victim of progressive education, which is responsible for courses like Contemporary Problems. This course can consist of just about anything—even of me. I was stunned recently to find that I have been anthologized in a textbook. The editors bought an article of mine on country music that was published in *Harper's* a few years ago. Even more incredible than the academic use of such an article is the list of "homework" questions at the end of it. One of them asks: "Why did the author wait until the end of the article before revealing her own tastes in music?" implying that there was a deep intellectual reason for my choice of sequence. The correct answer is: "Because she forgot to mention it earlier and she didn't feel like retyping."

It is such trends in education as this that account for the Cockerel's dearth of real knowledge, which makes him terribly boring after a time.

I also have no wish to be in bed with a man who has to leave me in order to do his homework, only to have the homework turn out to be *me*.

People my age have certain habits and knee-jerk reactions that make the Cockerel furious. If you say "ma'am" and "sir" to old or distinguished people, or if you greet cordially people you are known to dislike, the Cockerel will light into you.

"That's sick."

"You have to be polite."

"Like I mean why?"

"Because you must. It's right."

"That's a value judgment."

"That's a valuable judgment."

"Like you're a fascist."

Calling people fascists simply because they are not exactly like him is the Cockerel at his worst. His quick accusations of fascism are a projection. His lack of direction and his consequent yearning for a godlike leader are so great that he secretly fears fascistic tendencies in himself, and so he must pin the rose on someone else. Despite his flaming liberalism, he may be our most dangerous citizen.

The Cockerel is a perfect Carry Nation about drinking. He may have a beer with chili, but otherwise he is a smug teetotaler with an especially visceral hatred for martinis. Confused reformers are always anti-martini. It is the Establishment drink, the Wall Street drink, the drink of brittle, memsahibish women. The martini reminds the Cockerel of imperialism because it was invented by accident in India by a British officer's houseboy who got the decanters mixed up. The sun has been setting on the martini ever since, but if the Cockerel had his way, he would outlaw it. It is this more than anything else that puts enmity between the Cockerel and me, because women my age are card-carrying members of the Martini Generation.

He is also anti-tobacco. "Like how can you smoke those things? I mean like your lungs must be black, like." I am used to the kind of man who carries a lighter even though he doesn't smoke, in case he finds himself with a woman who does. The Cockerel carries brochures with pictures of somebody's lungs in a jar.

He wants to ban my pleasures, but he thinks his own should be legalized. When he is turned on, his conversation gets stranger than ever.

"Like how do we *know* that we're speaking English? I mean, we *think* we are, but how can we tell, like?"

"We're speaking English because we're speaking English."

"Like do you have to be so judgmental? How do you *know* we're speaking English? Couldn't it be an illusion?"

"What *are* you getting at?"

"Are we, you know, like in the room, or is the room in us? I mean, there are no absolutes."

There is another course at Cockerel U. called Situation Ethics. They study all about where the room is.

Now that men have been humanized, they have dreamed up new tortures. I thwart the Sensuous Man because I am simply not a toucher. In bed, yes, but not in public.

When the Sensuous Man lights a woman's cigarette, he expects her to cup his hand. It took me a long time to realize this. I knew from his vague air of disappointment that I was doing something wrong, but I couldn't imagine what it was, except perhaps smoking too much. Finally I learned that it was something I was *not* doing when a Sensuous Man who had just lit my cigarette smiled sadly and said, "You know, you're the only woman I ever did that for who didn't cup my hand."

A corollary to hand-cupping is thigh-touching. It works like this. You are sitting next to a man in a restaurant or in a car, and he asks you if you want something—more wine, a rest stop. As you answer, you are supposed to put your hand lightly on his thigh and let your fingers trail there for a moment. Not too long and not too high up, just enough to let him know that *you* know he got a high score on the *How Sensuous Are You?* quiz.

The woman who does not cup hands, touch thighs, or rub backs reminds the Sensuous Man of his "old" image that the media have ordered him to slough off. To him, she is all the things that traditionalist man is accused of being: stiff, formal, stoic, cold, inhuman, etc., so he may get very hostile and ask aggressive questions like, "Why are you so uptight?" Sometimes I think he's getting touched in the head.

The Sensuous Man is always trying to prove what a male chauvinist he is *not*. Anything that makes him seem humanized and liberated is grist for his mill. One of his favorite tricks is to circulate at cocktail parties saying, "I can't get it up" to every woman he meets. The merry claim of impotence makes him seem soft, so to speak. It is also very useful in another way. It is a surefire method of acquiring a new girl friend without going to the trouble of courting her in that nasty old aggressive (read unsensuous) way. Now that so many women pride themselves on their sexual expertise, the impotent man has become, incredibly, a real catch. The woman who takes him home and works over him has a chance to be the first girl on the block to get him hard. She can test her new fellatio techniques and find out where she blows on a scale of one to ten.

The Sensuous Man is always bragging about how sexually secure he is. With a jaunty, confident smile, he tells a woman that he uses Johnson's Baby Shampoo. Next he confesses that he shaves under his arms. "Deodorant works better if you do," he says. "After all, why shouldn't a man shave under his arms? There's nothing wrong with that. Some men might not be liberated enough to do it, but it doesn't worry me a bit. I'm not afraid of being 'effeminate.' "

There is nothing, really, that a woman can say at such moments. "I think that's wonderful" is too fervent for a discussion of armpits. All you can say is, "Oh, do you?"

"Yes," he says, "and do you know something else?"

Oh, God, what's coming now? Electrolysis in his crack?

This is when he tells you that he cries.

Going to bed with the Sensuous Man is exhausting, not because he is an accomplished stick man, but because he likes a woman to undress him. He just lies there while you pull and tug. When a man undresses a woman he feels like a rogue; when a woman undresses a man she feels like an undertaker. If a man can't work a hook-and-eye or a garter, a woman can laugh throatily and say, "Let *me* do it, silly," and sound very sexy. When a man says something like this he merely sounds dippy.

He insists upon trying new techniques that are supposed to make wonderful experiences even more wonderful. He makes a woman hold an ice cube in her mouth while she goes down on him. Maybe Xaviera Hollander can bring expertise to such acts, but I can't. I swallowed the ice cube. *Why* can't we forget all this nonsense and go back to plain old frenching, like at Ole Miss?

Every man wants a woman to play with his penis. The Sensuous Man wants her to play with his testicles. The trouble is, most women are scared silly of testicles because we grew up hearing chilling tales about how fragile they are. There was the story of the little boy who had mumps that "went down on him." Worst of all is that conversation that every daughter has with her father. Even the most reticent father will launch this conversation because he feels it is his duty. Shortly after a girl begins to develop, her father draws her aside for the "You Can Cripple a Man for Life" seminar. "If a man ever tries to force himself on you, I want you to promise me that you'll kick him where it hurts. You know where I mean, don't you? You don't? Well, ask your mother. Anyway, that's where I want you to kick him. If a man is kicked there, he'll think twice before he tries to force himself on another girl. Take my word for it."

When the Sensuous Man gently takes my hand and guides it to his testicles, I always feel like the Cartier diamond cutter working at his trade in the back seat of a Lincoln being driven around the streets of New York. That place is full of potholes.

In the fifties we had our deathless dialogues. The seventies deathless dialogue revolves around testicle play.

"Don't be afraid, they won't hurt you."

"I'm afraid I'll hurt *them.*"

"No you won't."

"You can cripple a man for life this way."

"There's a ridge down there, like a piece of string. Tickle it."

"Am I hurting you?"

"No! Look, will you stop holding them like an egg?"

Haec sunt mea ornamenta, as the mother of the Gracchi said.

11

REGULAR GUY-ISM
or The "Different" Man
Faces Life

America is a land of regular guys. For every man who has been
humanized or sensitized, there are thousands upon thousands
who dwell in a perpetual fraternity party of the spirit. They are
frequently unhappy, but the different man is unhappier still
because Americans make life much harder for the nonconformist male than for the nonconformist female. The woman who
is different can cultivate her difference into mystery, which is
very sexy. People say of her, "Still waters run deep," which
means she goes off like a bomb the moment she hits a mattress.
But to say "Still waters run deep" of a man merely makes him
sound furtive.

Social pressures force all but the strongest different men into
introverted personality patterns. They are usually quiet, neat,
and well organized—virtues to be sure, but not *male* virtues in
the eyes of All-American dips like Ma Perkins, the heartland
landlady. She is the different man's foremost nemesis.

Anyone who has known lean days, like free-lance writers, is
familiar with Mrs. Perkins. She can be found in small cities like
Worcester, Mobile, and Boise, whenever resourceful widows
inherit huge houses. A typical Ma Perkins ad reads like a cue

card for a Cotton Mather sermon: *Clean studio, quiet house, conv. to churches, non-drinker, no pets.*

Life is bleak chez Perkins, but only for female tenants. She expects women to turn everything off at ten P.M., from their radios to their life-support systems, but her male tenants can get away with anything because she is America's foremost champion of Regular Guy-ism. She expects the worst from men, and if she doesn't get it she wonders if they are "a little funny." To her way of thinking, men are born-free barbarians who change their sheets once a year and throw food. Her dream man is Oscar Madison. Any man who does not have a pile of dirty laundry in the middle of the floor at all times is not "normal." He is not a regular guy, therefore, he bears watching.

I once roomed with a Mrs. Perkins who was convinced that a very nice loner-type insurance man who lived across the hall from me was none other than STOCKING MURDERER STILL AT LARGE. "It stands to reason," she told me. "He's as neat as a pin and he subscribes to *The National Geographic.*" We were in the *Playboy* era but Mrs. Perkins still had a thing on *The National Geographic.* To her, it was the magazine for perverts because it contained pictures of bare-breasted African women. She would not have been disturbed to find copies of real girlie magazines in my neighbor's apartment—provided they were strewn all over the room—because regular guys read girlie magazines. But when she found three years' worth of *Geographics* stacked neatly by date, she panicked.

Her fears were increased by the fact that my quiet neighbor's name was Claude.

"Pzzzzt!" she hissed at me one afternoon from behind her beaded curtains.

"Yes, ma'am?"

"Don't you think it's funny that his name is Claude? What kind of a name is that for a man?"

Proponents of Regular Guy-ism believe that men should be

named Bill or Joe or Dick. In her bat-brained way, Mrs. Perkins had a point: people are shaped by their names, and in a nation committed to Regular Guy-ism, any man named Claude is bound to feel a bit different. Eventually they become Claude-like and start doing Claudian things like folding their laundry, washing their dishes, and collating their *Geographics*.

Mrs. Perkins began to keep tabs on Claude, and started a list of his comings and goings. It was a very short list because Claude was a homebody.

"Pzzzt!" she hissed at me. "I'm *sure* he's the stocking murderer now."

"What makes you think so?"

"It stands to reason. He never goes out."

Women like Mrs. Perkins hold two diametrically opposed views of the male sex. They believe that men should be tamed and domesticated by a good woman, yet at the same time, they believe that normal men have a streak of wildness. Although she was a teetotaler, she expected men to go out to taverns and get into fights and come home roaring drunk. Men who voluntarily stay home nights are not regular guys.

Claude's subdued life-style began to get to Mrs. Perkins in a serious way. She started going through his garbage, and she found more and more excuses to go up to his apartment. One night when she took him a new curtain rod, she found him eating dinner.

The next day:

"Pzzzt!"

The beaded curtains parted to reveal a frantically beckoning finger.

"You should have seen the little-bitty dinner he had fixed. A little-bitty hamburger patty, a spoonful of beans, and a little-bitty dish of fruit cocktail. What kind of a dinner is that for a *man?* I like a man who likes to hunker down and really *eat*, don't you?"

"Oh, yes," I said happily.

This encouraged her to reminisce about her girlhood on a wheat ranch, and all the hearty trenchermen who worked as hired hands for her father. She and her mother had cooked for them, and it was a joy to see healthy, happy, normal men putting away four pork chops and half a loaf of bread apiece.

Claude's table manners had also upset her.

"He had a linen place mat, *and* a matching napkin, *and* he was wiping his mouth just as nice as you please." She put her hands on her enormous hips and gave a little sissy shake. It was a dreadful sight. "I tell you, there's something wrong with that boy. He's peculiar. A normal man eats like he means it!" she exclaimed in a burst of joyous nostalgia, obviously thinking about the ranch hands who had wiped their mouths on their sleeves.

Meanwhile, the stocking murderer was still at large. Mrs. Perkins grew more and more dippy with each attack. Her theory of the Regular Guy and the messes he makes drove her like one possessed to inspect Claude's apartment while he was at work, hoping against hope to find a pile of spaghetti in the middle of the table or a pickle on the sofa arm. I stayed home all day writing true confessions, so I could hear every time she sneaked in with her pass key.

Hearing so much from Mrs. Perkins about what normal men do was starting to have an effect on me: I began to think more and more about something else that normal men do that she hadn't mentioned. I hadn't had a man for a long time; not since I had moved to Perkins Arms, in fact. I couldn't bring one home because she had already told me in a long, euphemistic speech that she didn't allow that sort of thing. However, there was a perfectly good in-house lover available. I found Claude attractive in an underweight, ascetic sort of way. I knew perfectly well he wasn't the stocking murderer, and my instincts told me he wasn't gay. I knew he was shy, but that has its charms. As

for his loner tendencies, I saw a logical explanation for them
that was not at all menacing. He was a stranger in town, a
trainee in a company that paid trainees peanuts, and that, like
most insurance companies, forbade "fraternization" between
male and female employees. I had worked for them through a
temp agency for a week, so I knew what a dismal place it was.
Obviously, Claude knew no girls to take out, and could not
afford to date. It all added up to the distinct possibility that he
was as sexually overdue as I was.

Mrs. Perkins, on the other hand, had a dazzling social life:
the Altar Society, the DAR, and Bingo Night. One day when I
thought I would go mad if I didn't have It, I decided to try and
seduce Claude. I waited until Mrs. Perkins was out of the
house, took a bath with White Shoulders bath oil, and left the
top three buttons of my blouse undone. I placed myself in the
hall when Claude was due home, and when I heard him round
the corner of the hall, I bent over and pretended to straighten
my door mat.

I was right, he was shy. I had to come on stronger than I like
to do, but it worked. Hearing that Mrs. Perkins was out for the
evening, Claude went and bought some beer. We drank it amid
the *National Geographic*s and an hour or so later we were in bed.

Once he got going, he was terrific. Like so many different
men, he had a lot saved up. He also had a dark side to his
moon, not enough to make him a stocking murderer, but
enough to give him a talent for some of the more pleasant
aspects of obscenity. The Regular Guy is so obsessed by his
own normalness that his lovemaking tends to be depressingly
standardized. He enjoys unusual practices as long as they are
confined to stag movies, but he avoids them in real life, unless
he is with a prostitute who makes it clear beforehand that such-
and-such is her specialty. The businesslike arrangement up
front takes the onus off what he calls "something really weird."
When that weird something is called a specialty, the Regular

Guy feels soothed, because being a *specialist* is part of the American Dream.

The different man, on the other hand, can accept so-called abnormality because he himself has been called abnormal so many times. Being an introvert also gives him time to think, to explore the facets of his personality and to plumb the depths of his sexuality—things that are impossible to do on the golf course. Sometimes he is "a little funny" when measured against the Regular Guy norm, but he is also lots of fun.

The writer's boundless curiosity and lust for experience gives us a dark side of the moon, too, so life chez Perkins became the dark at the top of the stairs.

It was bound to happen. One night the DAR broke up early. Claude and I were so involved in what we were doing that we didn't hear Mrs. Perkins creeping up the stairs. Suddenly, the door burst open and there she was. I was sprawled across the bed with her best Sears spring-flowers sofa bolster under my stomach, there was an opened jar of cold cream on the table, and Claude was hunched over me on all fours like an incubus in a medieval witchcraft drawing.

In her horrified brain, only one thing made sense.

"Homosexuals!" she screamed.

I guess she thought it stood to reason.

It stands to reason that America's love affair with Regular Guy-ism can cause the different man serious trouble, because dips like Mrs. Perkins frequently take their suspicions to the police. Policemen have to investigate such charges no matter how silly they might be, and to make matters worse, most policemen are themselves regular guys. They do not like the Claudes of America, so life can be perilous or even tragic for the introverted man. The standard media phrase for an alleged murderer or child molester is: "The suspect was described as a loner who kept to himself." This is often enough to make any different man a pariah in the eyes of his neighbors.

I sometimes shudder to think what my life would be like if I were a forty-two-year-old bachelor instead of a forty-two-year-old spinster. But if I were, I wouldn't dare do some of the things I now do without a qualm—like roaming up and down the alley with a bag of Little Friskies ululating, "See what I've got for you!" I am known in my neighborhood as the "cat lady," but whoever heard of a cat man? The cops would hear about him very quickly, especially if he were wearing a raincoat. Because I am a woman, and an unmarried one at that, people are willing and even eager to shrug off my idiosyncrasies with: "Oh, well, she's probably sex-starved." No one shrugs off idiosyncratic sex-starved men.

Regular-Guyism has created the pseudo-sports freak. Intellectuals and feminists frequently decry the popularity of spectator sports among American men, implying that *all* men are hopelessly mired in macho violence. A great many men merely pretend to like sports out of a fear of seeming different. The real sports fan is the lower-class Archie Bunker type who sits in front of the television set drinking beer and eating potato chips for two solid days. Sports mean everything to such men because their conception of masculinity is bound up with brutal, mindless physical force. The pseudo-sports freak is the upper-class, well-educated suburban professional man. He doesn't need to associate masculinity with physical brutality because he has other masculine perks such as money and job power, yet he spends the weekend in front of the television set, too. A married friend of mine who lives in the most expensive suburb in America told me that she refuses all invitations to weekend neighborhood cocktail parties because it depresses her to see such men force themselves into the Regular-Guy mold. When the big game comes on, they all go into the solid mahogany, genuine leather den and get sloshed on Beefeater martinis while they cheer their troglodytic polar opposites.

The pseudo-sports freak is like the pseudo-Hemingway fan. Many men, when asked to name their favorite author, quickly— too quickly—say "Hemingway." He is the author for Regular Guys. They don't dare *not* like him.

The womanish man is not a homosexual but simply a man who would have been better off had he been born female. The conflict between his technical masculinity and his psychological femininity keeps him off-balance so that he becomes high-strung, waspish, and irascible. He is a male bitch.

It is said that a woman never knows a man until she marries him. I say a woman never knows a man until she works for him. One of the most trying periods in my life was my tenure as executive assistant to Ronald Cutler Lacey III, who refused to be first on the telephone.

"Get him on the phone first and make him wait a minute or so, *then* tell me."

I am just not good at this sort of thing. Diplomacy is not my long suit and serpentine games get on my nerves. I also have one really endearing trait: I never stay mad, and I don't mind in the least being the first to speak after a fight. Mr. Lacey had the memory of an elephant and he could pout even longer than Leah Lee Blumenthal, a girl I knew in Memphis who was both a Southern belle and a Jewish princess all rolled into one.

On day I said, "Mr. Farley is on line two."

"Oh, he *is*, is he? Well, he can just *stay* on line two forever for all *I* care. I'll never speak to that man again as long as I live. He's a terrible person, a really wretched individual, the sort who takes advantage of every good quality he finds. I'm the soul of patience as you know, but my patience is now at an end."

The light on line two started to look like an angry eye to me. My stomach knotted up into little fists of tension and I started to sweat, but Mr. Lacey talked on.

"If he thinks he can send me a contract like that, he's got another thought coming. I won't have that contract in this office. It's a disgrace, the most unprofessional attempt at manipulation I've ever seen. I wash my hands of it! So now he wants to talk to me, does he? *Well*, I don't want to talk to *him*."

Mr. Lacey had a Pilate-like tendency to wash his hands loud and clear over at least three matters per day. He also had a unique and very dramatic way of disposing of his enemies. Sometimes when a Wretched Individual tried to reach him by phone, he would rise from his chair and arc his eyebrows in a silent-movie expression denoting disbelief and say: "He no longer exists. I have *erased* him! I do not acknowledge his existence. As far as I'm concerned, he never *was*."

The floor was littered with imaginary grease spots, the sole mortal remains of Wretched Individuals whom Mr. Lacey had dropped into the acid vats of his mind. I also had to cope with an ever-growing list of people whose "name shall not be mentioned in this office." One of the names was that of his son. "When I think of the sacrifices I made for you-know-who, and for what? Did he appreciate me? No. The last time I called him at Princeton, the night before he enlisted in the Peace Corps, he *hung up on me*. We laugh at expressions like 'serpent's tooth,' but how apt! Oh, how apt!"

Mrs. Lacey lived on vodka and Librium. I dreaded the times when I had to call her and give her a message because all I could get out of her was a sound something like, "Ong-a-oo." Each time I had to go back to the very beginning and explain who I was and where I worked. When I gave her the message she would say, "Ong-a-oo . . . please . . . where . . . no pencil . . . oh, frig it . . . ong-a-oo." Our elliptical conversations were not helped by the deafening blast of Sousa marches from her stereo. I suppose she was reaching in desperation for masculinity.

The womanish man has one great value: he is somebody to bitch to. Bitching to another woman is usually not satisfying because she tends to get very calm and superior, as if to prove that while *you* may be bitchy, *she* is not. She always tries to say something nice about the person you want to run down, and maintains an air of "We must try to look for the good in people."

The womanish man is always ready to run anybody down, even people he doesn't know. At these moments he is a good listener. Tell him the worst about a roommate or a lover and he will roll his eyes, purse his mouth, click his tongue, and exclaim, "Oh, you don't *mean* it!" at precisely the right moments. No matter whom you bitch about, it always reminds him of his own current wretch. "It's Farley all *over* again. Birds of a feather. I *hate* petty people, don't you? If I were you, I would just *erase* her. Just erase her! I mean, there's no forgiving people like that, is there? You know, the trouble with you is, you're too agreeable—just like me. I endure things like this all the time. It doesn't pay to be kind and thoughtful and easygoing, does it? *I* know. Oh, do I know!"

At times the womanish man can be a positive relief from Regular Guy-ism. Any woman who has dated many lawyers or engineers knows that sinking feeling when a man interrupts her diatribes with: "Now, let's look at this logically." Looking at things logically, also known as "going to the heart of the matter," can be oppressive to the spirit. The American Regular Guy feels compelled to come on like a lawyer whether he's a lawyer or not. Logic and deductive reasoning are so thoroughly associated with masculinity that even men in hang-loose creative fields voluntarily put these clamps on themselves, especially when they are with a woman.

The womanish man hates logic. It cramps his style. One day

Mr. Lacey took me to lunch and his foremost Wretched Person walked into the restaurant and sat down at a table across from us. I skittered nervously but Mr. Lacey patted my hand and shook his head. "He's not really here," he told me, and gave a sublime smile. Then I remembered that the foremost Wretched Person no longer walked the face of this *earth*, so he could not possibly have walked into the restaurant. He had been erased two days before.

Nothing upsets the applecart of Regular Guy-ism more than a really complex, enigmatic man. We believe that men should be simple. It's all right for an Italian man to have a fine Italian hand, but the American man must be easy to psych out. To us, simplicity is a measure of masculinity just as complexity is a measure of femininity.

Americans derive so much sexual security from this state of affairs that it seriously affects our political situation. As long as Our Leader is one-dimensional we feel safe, no matter how stupid he may be. This is why we never turned a hair back in the days when Eisenhower kept saying "Gosh." The subtle, complicated Adlai Stevenson was twice defeated by the politics of Gosh, which made Americans happy and at peace with themselves.

On the other hand, 1963–1974 proved to be a tumultuous eleven years because the moment a complex man takes office we have a national nervous breakdown.

Lyndon Johnson and Richard Nixon were a pair of un-fathomable Druids who between them managed to drive America crazy. Like Stonehenge, they could not be explained; they were just *there*. Living through their administrations was like going back in time to Celtic Gaul when black-robed priests practiced government-by-full-moon and consigned their enemies to the slaughter stone. Like all Druid priests, Johnson liked to perform sudden mysterious rituals such as pulling dogs' ears, exposing knife scars, and touching the groin. Things like this make the hoi polloi nervous and keep them wondering. Johnson did not wear a black hood but he did a lot of Druid-like bawling and howling on the campaign trail, and he wore rimless spectacles that invariably caught the light and bounced it back at his television audiences, so that he seemed all-seeing but unseen.

The High Priest Nixon guarded the secrets of his administration and personality with the same zeal that Druids of eld used to guard their Ogam alphabet. The Oval Oak Grove was the scene of time-honored Druidic practices such as weeping, praying, and making human sacrificial offerings. Nixon appeared to be the kind of person who counted time by nights instead of days in the Druid custom; he also played threnodic tunes in the wee hours and prefaced each cryptic Druidic oration with the announcement that soon everything would be perfectly clear.

Each of our Druids had his own personal adjective: "crafty" and "tricky." The words obsessed us as much as the men themselves. Analyzing their personalities turned into a masochistic national game; no one could rest until these male enigmas had been explained. Books poured forth, all about childhood diseases and old girl friends. No autobiographical clue was too minor to be weighed because we cannot bear to let a complex man slip through our national fingers. We *must* psych him out, find the key to his personality and unlock the mystery, so that he can be rendered safely one-dimensional.

America is no place for complex men. We make them miserable. Johnson was too sui generis to care if people hated him, but the much more conformist Nixon did care. He wanted more than anything else to be a Regular Guy, and his efforts to hide his complexity only made people hate him more. If he had gone for broke and given free and unashamed rein to his twists and turns and convolutions, he could have achieved a certain Borgia-like dignified menace. But the forced warmth he attempted only made him more puzzling and hence more threatening.

Nixon was a social rather than a political tragedy. It just so happened that one led to the other.

Our distrust of complex men raises a serious question: Is America destined to go to hell in a bucket of Regular Guy-ism? We need a Disraeli, but could we *take* a Disraeli? Would a brilliant, subtle statesman with many skeins to his personality pattern drive us crazy? Do we perhaps have a deep psychological need for just-plain-folks pols whose philosophical limit is "Life is unfair"?

The naiveté of American leaders, which Alexander Solzhenitsyn says is the laughingstock of Kremlin diplomats, is really Regular Guy-ism, the politics of Gosh.

12

THE BORN-AGAIN BOYS
or Simplistic Men

Just as the Forty-Niner need not be forty-nine, the Born-Again man need not be a Fundamentalist or even religious. It is a back-to-the-basics, black-and-white state of mind. The Born-Again man can be found in any unsophisticated American hinterland from northern New England to Washington's Olympic Peninsula, but he is best represented by the Southerner.

Having mentioned Fundamentalists, I cannot resist the temptation to divide the Born-Again man into two types: the High Born-Again and the Low Born-Again. My most memorable High Born-Again lover was named Clyde.

Clyde had been raised a Fundamentalist and baptized with full submersion rites in a river, but it didn't "take," as he put it. Unlike most men of his type, he was a natty dresser, sometimes a little too natty. He had an avocado-green suit that belonged at a racetrack—but then he spent quite a lot of time at the racetrack. I drink, smoke, fornicate, and dance, but I won't gamble. Clyde drank, smoked, fornicated, and gambled, but he wouldn't dance. We did not always find mutually agreeable pastimes, but we understood each other. The Protestant mind always condemns *one* sin, generally the one that does not appeal to us in the first place, or the one that we are not very good at. Gambling doesn't appeal to me, and Clyde had no sense of rhythm, so he had his official sin and I had mine. We compromised by spending most of our time fornicating.

Unlike the Roman Catholic man, who often hates sex and views women as an "occasion of sin," the Born-Again man, whether religious or not, believes that every word in the Bible is the literal truth. God said to do it, so they do it. Rural at heart, they look upon sex the way they look upon sunlight, rain, and horse manure: it's good.

They are good at it, too. Some of these down-home country boys are positive jackrabbits. Once when Clyde had lasted half an hour, I had to stop him; I just couldn't take any more. Their ambition is to "make a girl sore," but this goal does not involve sadism. It is simply their yardstick of success. On a scale of one to ten, Clyde was an eleven.

The Born-Again man loves cunnilingus. Sometimes, as in Clyde's case, his devotion to this act approaches obsession. Men like Clyde are often much less racially prejudiced than many urbane sophisticates because they have known so many blacks and even worked alongside them, but they are still guided by the Southern man's fixed idea that white women must be worshiped. However, he knows that if he worships a white woman *too* much he would never be able to enjoy her sexually, so he has devised a compromise: he goes down on her constantly. The expression "to go down" is indicative of his attitude; it suggests obeisance and kneeling. Often he literally kneels. The usual position for cunnilingus, with the woman lying on her back in a bed, is not nearly enough for him. He likes to do it while she sits in a chair and he kneels on the floor. He also likes to place her on a table, an altarlike approach of which he is especially fond. This is why Clyde, who cared nothing for home decor, spent a small fortune on a butcher-block coffee table. He wanted something "good and strong," as he explained, because his preferences in women tended toward the Junoesque.

Clyde was a self-proclaimed expert at judging the difference between a woman who is merely "nooky" and that select group he called—naturally—"table nooky." He swore that he could take one look at any fully clothed woman and know immediately in which category she belonged. This was his favorite pastime in public places. One day in a crowded restaurant, he stopped suddenly in the middle of a sentence and gestured at a woman who had just sat down.

"See that gal over there in the green dress?"

"Yes. What about her?"

"She's not table nooky."

"How do you know? Is she a friend of yours?"

"Never saw her before in my life," he said proudly.

"Then how can you tell?"

"I just can, that's all." He shrugged. "She's good nooky but she's not table nooky."

As much as Clyde adored cunnilingus, he was not the best practitioner I have ever run into because he talked while he did it. It had a staccato effect on my "mounting pleasure," as they say in novels. The moment I felt a climax approaching and started to move, Clyde would stop, look up with a happy smile, and say, "Do you like that? Does that feel good? Am I pleasurin' you?"

Clyde was an archconservative and a dedicated patriot. Sometimes I think that he was attracted to me because I knew all the words to the only song to come out of the Spanish-American War, "Just Break the News to Mother." He was always asking me to sing it for him, and when I did he got tears in his eyes. Once, around midnight, we were in bed and at the foreplay stage when the station on the radio signed off with "The Star-Spangled Banner." Clyde stopped what he was doing until it was over.

He liked to read and was especially fond of Ayn Rand. I served in a backup capacity when he read *The Fountainhead:*

"Honey, what's this-here thing, I-o-n-i-c column?" He also liked Taylor Caldwell, whose frequent calls for the return of the masculine principle in politics pleased him much. I tried to explain that by masculinity she meant *virtus* in the old Roman sense, but my explanation, like Clyde's baptism, did not "take." He thought she was telling him to go out and buy another gun.

Low Born-Again Men? They are Dwayne and Dewey, the mudguard twins. They are the men George Gilder means when he refers to "unsocialized males," except that he puts it too mildly. To paraphrase a line from *I, Claudius*, Dwayne and Dewey "could wreck the country merely by strolling through it."

Dwayne and Dewey live for and through their cars. One seldom sees *all* of Dwayne and Dewey, just their jean-clad legs sticking out from under a car. This is where they seem to spend most of their time. I have never figured out what it is they do under there; it couldn't possibly be repair work because their cars are always total wrecks. I think they have substituted the crankcase for the vulva, and simply lie underneath the car staring up into it, a kind of beaver shot for men who like cars better than women.

Dangling from the rearview mirror are a pair of huge felt dice and a topless kewpie doll that someone won at a shooting gallery at the county fair. The glove compartment is notable for its absence; there's just a hole where it used to be. The window rollers have been torn off. The seats are full of what look like gopher holes. There is no glass in the rear window. The back seat contains scattered shotgun shells, crumpled newspapers, and lots of stains. Shining like a precious jewel in this tarnished crown is the CB radio.

There is a certain kind of ostensibly sophisticated but extremely parochial New Yorker who does not really believe that Dwayne and Dewey exist. Intellectually, the New Yorker knows the mudguard twins are out there somewhere, but emotionally he cannot take them in. The avant garde woman in a poncho who lives in the Village is such a New Yorker. I knew such a woman in 1967. She constantly said things like: "Everybody I know is for gun control." She was convinced that Eugene McCarthy would win the Democratic nomination by acclamation and go on to carry every state in the election because: "Everybody I know is for McCarthy." Such New Yorkers do not know Dwayne and Dewey.

Although Dwayne and Dewey generally do not bother to vote, they exert an influence on hinterland political climates. They are among the chief architects of Wasteland America. The presence of destructive men in such places leads to overreactive law-and-order police forces, hard-line preachers, despairing women of the "Mama Tried" type, and hypocritical, desperate liquor laws. Such atmospheres lead in turn to hopelessness, paranoia, and a ferocious right-wing, us-against-the-world attitude that defeats true conservatism as much as it defeats liberalism.

It is not necessary to meet Dwayne and Dewey to know them. Traveling through their bailiwicks, one senses their spirit everywhere even though they themselves may be safely locked up in the pokey. In *The Wounded Land*, Hans Habe noted the Dwayne and Dewey "feel" of some of the places he visited. He observed that "the South is not characteristic of America, but it is the most characteristic bit," and went on to describe the kind of sad cafe where Dwayne and Dewey consume their Twinkies and strawberry pop:

> The lunch counters with their plank walls, their small meshed mosquito nets, to which insects cling like escaping prisoners caught in the barbed wire, dingy white, black and white, no other color, the complete absence of any color, the jukeboxes, the stale, crumbling cakes under glass domes to which the flies cling like famished prisoners, the thin coffee,

menu cards beneath tattered celluloid, paper napkins in rusty dispensers, slot machines empty of cigarettes or candy bars, the kind of tin cutlery which one finds in prisons. And the people—traveling salesmen in shirt sleeves and rolled ankle socks, mannish girls in blue jeans, landlords who looked as though they had slept in their clothes, waitresses who looked as though they had just been rescued from drowning. And whiskey, whiskey, whiskey as the only consolation and sex, sex, sex, because here there is nothing except sex and whiskey, whiskey and sex. Over everything a brooding, brutish, evil silence, the stifling atmosphere of misery, inferiority and resentment.

I can go Habe one better. A friend and I once stopped at a Dwayne-and-Dewey-owned cafe with a flapping EAT sign. The proprietor, who was also the chef, nearly knocked us off the stools with his whiskey breath. His arms, and what we could see of his chest under his torn undershirt, were covered with tattoos—daggers dripping blood, swastikas, nude women with enormous black bushes of pubic hair, Iron Crosses, and coiled snakes. The specialty of the house was "Italian spaghetti," so we ordered it. The man took our orders in silence, then left the sad cafe and went into the grocery next door. He returned shortly with a bag containing two boxes of Chef Boy-Ar-Dee spaghetti dinners. As we watched, he cooked them according to the directions on the package.

This kind of atmosphere provokes so much alienation that the inevitable result is more Dwaynes and Deweys. It is a vicious circle—literally.

When Dwayne and Dewey sign off the CB band with "We gone," they are speaking a kind of truth. Their usefulness is gone. As long as there is a wilderness to be hacked or a frontier to be opened, Dwayne and Dewey are needed. When the frontier closes, they become a menace. I am a descendant of seventeenth-century Dwaynes and Deweys who were "transported to His Majesty's plantations in Virginia." Colonialism and imperialism siphoned off such men, got them out of nice countries and into big bad countries. Now we have no place left but outer space. One of these days, the moon will be dappled with flapping EAT and H-TEL signs.

When I lived in New Orleans, I had *one* date with a Dwayne-Dewey. Never mind how I met him; I have no intention of confessing everything. His name was Tabor Covington. Southern men of this type often have beautiful names. When I worked on a newspaper and covered a Ku Klux Klan rally, I heard the following orders issued by the Grand Klutz: "Hey, Raiford, grab that nigger! Langston, hold his arms! Beaufort, you and Lafayette kick him!"

I fully intended to go to bed with Tabor, but as things turned out it didn't happen. A great deal more *did* happen, because Dwayne-Dewey men cannot simply go to bed and be done with it. They like to build up sexual tension first. Their motto is: "Danger and death give an added filip."

Tabor called for me on his motorcycle and we went to his favorite bar for beer and crawfish. My first hint of what was to come came when he began to talk with great intensity about a murder that had taken place in the very bar where we were. He pointed out the place where the body had lain—right beside our table.

After our meal, we got back on the motorcycle and tore through town. I hung on for dear life, too terrified to scream or wonder what became of the little old ladies who scattered out of our way. With a bloodcurdling Rebel yell, Tabor tore into the entrance of Metairie Cemetery, careened around the huge, teethlike mausoleums, and screeched to a halt in front of the Confederate catacomb.

We went into the catacomb. I leaned against someone's tomb, which looked like a file drawer, my knees wobbling. Tabor pulled a pint of white lightning from his pocket and took a swig, then offered me the bottle. I took a swig for medicinal reasons. Three more nonmedicinal swigs later, I decided that everything was really perfectly all right, so off we went to Lake Pontchartrain amusement park.

At the park, Tabor hurled himself into frenetic activity. He rang the bell, shot the wooden ducks, pitched baseballs, threw darts, and tossed rings. Throughout all this, his eyes were glittering strangely. I assumed it was mere competition and a wish to win over the other men. I did not know that he was getting "juiced up" for our planned sexual activity.

He hit every game in the park, and I followed along behind him laden with "My Sweetheart" pillow cases and wooden hula dancers on sticks. From time to time we ducked behind a post and took more swigs of white lightning. Finally, we both got hungry so we had milk shakes and hot dogs.

"Let's ride the roller coaster!" he said.

As we stumbled up the ramp and collapsed into a seat, some unfortunate man accidentally brushed Tabor's elbow. That did it. He swung at the man, and they started fighting. The roller coaster took off. At the first sickening dip, I threw up—into the wind, of course. Tabor was still fighting. I threw up again. Everybody started screaming.

When the ride was over, Tabor knocked the man out, grabbed me, and took off through the crowds to where his motorcycle was parked. I remember wrapping my arms around his waist and experiencing a momentary sexual excitement, but then my head started spinning again. Tabor took off with another Rebel yell, raced through the moonlit night, and drove straight into Lake Pontchartrain.

The cops came and arrested Tabor. In the confusion of trying to raise the motorcycle, they did not notice me lying on the sand like a beached seal. I stumbled off to the nearest comfort station and did what I could with my appearance, then quietly slunk away and got a cab back home.

13

THE WOMAN'S MAN
or An Extreme of Unction

"This is Aldo. He is not tall, he is not pretty, he is not powerful, but Aldo knows what women like."

Next to Morris the Cat, Aldo Cella of the Lambrusco wine commercials represents advertising psychology at its finest.

There is a certain kind of man of whom other men say, "Whatever he's got, it's not showing" and "What does he *do* to them?" He is the man who could have Agrippina eating out of his hand in five minutes, the man who could make Catherine de Medici giggle. He is the Balmoral gamekeeper, John Brown, who could say things like, "Hold up your silly parasol, woman!" to Queen Victoria and get away with it. He is Sergeant Earl Miller of the New York State Troopers, who had the means to make Eleanor Roosevelt positively girlish. In short, he is the woman's man.

When men who lack his magic ask a woman, "What is that guy's secret?" she always says, "There's just something about him ..." This unfinished sentence is always accompanied by a kind of twisting, curling, kittenish body movement. She wraps her legs around each other, folds her arms, cups her elbows with her palms, and gives a little squeeze that makes her bosom swell out. "He's just so ..." she begins, and then breaks off with a giggle.

The resentful male supposition, "Whatever he's got, it's not showing," implies that the woman's man has been wonderfully endowed by Nature. I wouldn't know; I have known three woman's men in my life and I never slept with any of them. Ironically, this is often the case. A woman feels subconsciously that such a man is to be cherished. She fears that the thread of hostility that laces the tapestry of physical sex will spoil everything; she does not want to see his clay feet. Physical sex would also spoil the flirtations that the woman's man is so good at. He can infuse the simplest conversation with so much electricity and so many undercurrents that sex would be an anticlimax. Flirtation is frustration made pleasant; once the frustration is removed, the pleasantness tends to go with it. Most of all, a woman declines to sleep with a woman's man because she does not want to waste him. There are plenty of men to sleep with, but only a woman's man can *understand* her.

The genius he brings to female psychology makes him a priceless asset to companies that employ large numbers of women. His way with women is such that it sometimes helps to insure his own job. Often he is a man who has been kicked upstairs and given a noble but meaningless title like Executive Coordinator. Translated into Men's Washroomese it means: "He keeps the women happy."

I met one of my woman's men when I worked on a Southern newspaper. No one knew exactly what he did, but he did it beautifully. At one time he had been an editorial writer, but he tended to ignore topics like NATO in favor of tributes to the scarlet tanager, so he was given other duties. One of them was "belling the cats."

In an office full of male chauvinists, the Hen's Pen, as the Woman's Department was called, was literally a pen. There was a wall around us to separate us from the rest of the newsroom. The copy boys were not permitted to work for us. We had to walk all the way around the wall to the pneu tubes and send up our own copy. The only thing our office was convenient to was the men's room. The reporters used to cut through the Hen's Pen to save time. On their way back to their desks, they were often still zipping up their flies or rearranging their equipment inside their pants. We used to mutter, "Dress left, dress!" as they passed by.

Given such an atmosphere, morale in the Hen's Pen was frequently at rock bottom. Our balm in this Gilead was Rob, a jack-of-all-trades and master of one: *us*. Rob was the official peacekeeper, a floating, flirting ambassador of goodwill who spent much of his time sitting on our desks, drinking coffee, and saying, "Oh, yes, I know just how you feel" at precisely timed intervals. He never really said anything specific and he seldom solved any problems, but he could bank the most shrewish fires and leave us in that boneless, nerveless state of placidity that one associates with brood mares.

Rob could not take his vacation in June because that was when the Woman's Department had a collective nervous breakdown. We were swamped with brides, and every one of them wanted *her* picture in the upper-left-hand corner. One day when I was doing layout, I found that I had to get forty-three brides into two pages full of ads. I blew up, which started a chain reaction: the Woman's Editor blew, then the Home Furnishings editor, followed by the Food editor, and finally, the typist. For a few seconds, the men in the newsroom froze in terror at the sight of five hysterical females. Then somebody said, "Go get Rob!" in a tone usually reserved for directives like "Call the police!"

The woman's man is the only kind of man who can unravel the tight knot of Granny's teachings in me. Of all the A Lady Never admonitions I grew up with, the injunction against emoting in public is the strongest. *Serenity* was Granny's watchword, which is why I always pretend that nothing is wrong when everything is wrong.

Mr. Finklestein changed all that. To many Gentile women, *any* Jewish man is a woman's man. The Protestant woman is especially susceptible because our Bible-oriented religion has filled our heads with visions of all-knowing patriarchs. To me, the Jewish man is Papa, seated in utter majesty at the head of the table whence he dispenses wisdom, justice, and loving discipline. No amount of Jewish-mother stories can change my mental picture: it is the *shiksa's* blind spot.

I got my job with Mr. Finklestein through a temporary help agency. I was supposed to stay only two weeks, but I ended up staying four months. All the women in the office were Gentiles, and our conversations usually revolved around our boss. "Isn't he *sweet?*" was the standard opener.

My platonic love affair with Mr. Finklestein started the morning he insisted upon giving me half of his doughnut, or to use his idiom, "a nice doughnut." Something about the way he cut and served it made me want to cry. He used just his fingertips, barely touching it, and put my half in the exact center of the napkin. A few days later, as I was unwrapping my lunch, he came out of his office and peered anxiously at it. It was a hot dog from a street-corner pushcart.

"Ecch!" said Mr. Finklestein. "What you should have is a nice sammich," and then called his favorite deli and ordered me one.

The nice sammich was such a cornerstone of Mr. Finklestein's philosophy that I soon forgot how to spell the word properly. I even started pronouncing it his way. When I stenciled a sign with THE EARL OF SAMMICH and put it on his door, he told me I was a "darling girl," had the sign framed, and added five hours to my time sheet.

In his dealings with other men, Mr. Finklestein was merci-

less. Whenever one of his salesmen complained about something, he would yell, "Listen! I don't want to hear your hard-
luck stories!" but if one of the office girls had a problem, he
would drop everything and apply the Finklestein stroke. He
could not get enough female problems to solve. As I sat typing
at my desk, I overheard the commiserations that went on in his
office. There would be a sob, followed by: "Here's a nice little
package of Kleenex. Keep it. You should always carry Kleenex.
Now look, it's only five days. That's nothing. You probably just
have a cold." One morning a girl rushed in with the news that
her apartment had been robbed, and Mr. Finklestein called
somebody he knew in the security business and bought her a
lock worthy of the Bastille.

I frustrated him because I did not cry on his shoulder. It just
so happened that my life was going extremely well for a change
while I worked for him. I had no men problems because there
was no man on the scene at that particular time. Having no sex
life, I did not get into any of the Dagwood-style messes that go
hand in hand with sex in my case. Absolutely nothing was
happening to me; the peace of celibacy was temporarily upon
me, and I was very happy.

It was a state of affairs that Mr. Finklestein simply could not
tolerate. He began to stop by my desk and probe for tragedy.
"How is it by you? You look tired. It's this heat. You probably
don't sleep so good, huh? Is your place air-conditioned? It isn't?
Do you have a nice fan?" I kept saying, "Oh, I'm fine, thanks,"
and Mr. Finklestein's face would fall. It went on like this until
that wonderful day when I cut my finger on the paper-slicer.

Mr. Finklestein sprang from his chair and grabbed his first-
aid kit—an understatement because it was as big as a suitcase.
He kept it on the wall, and in case anybody missed the point of
the red cross blazoned on the front, he had a sign under it:
FIRST-AID KIT!!

I had my finger in my mouth. Mr. Finklestein pulled it out

and washed it carefully in water, then proceeded to sterilize it. "Now some iodine. Stinging means curing. There. Now a nice bandage, flesh-colored so it shouldn't show."

His fat stubby fingers were incredibly deft as he worked over me and his little murmurings were oddly pleasant. After he had bandaged me up, he took me into his office and made me a cup of tea on his hot plate. I felt myself falling under his spell. I wanted to repay him in some way, to let him know how much I appreciated him. I knew the best thing I could do for him would be to tell him my troubles, but I didn't have any, so I made them up. Over the next few weeks, I poured out every imaginary agony I could dream up: an alcoholic father, a family history of cancer, a sister with an ectopic pregnancy, and a black-sheep brother whom I had not seen for ten years. Mr. Finklestein commiserated so beautifully that sometimes as I talked, I almost believed it all myself. He made me feel warm and secure and protected in a way I had never before felt. I would leave our sessions in that glow that women always feel after being stroked by a woman's man. One night I practically floated out the door, singing to myself and believing every word of it.

> *I've come to this great city*
> *To find a brother dear,*
> *And you would not dare insult me, sir,*
> *If Jack were only here!*

Mr. Finklestein was that type that Gentile women call "a nice little Jewish man." It sounds condescending and patronizing but it isn't; it is a term of the utmost affection and appreciation. A great many Jewish men are like him, especially Jewish bosses. Judging from an allusion he once made, I believe he operated on that Jewish idée fixe that every Gentile woman is beaten up every Saturday night. In his own way, Mr. Finklestein was trying to make up for all the swaggering, drunken Gentile fathers, husbands, and boyfriends that populated his unconscious mind.

One of the luckiest women in the world was Queen Victoria, who had a woman's man at her disposal during every stage of her long life. Her first was Lord Melbourne, her prime minister during the early part of her reign. Like so many men of this type, Melbourne had no power whatsoever over his own wife, the wild and wooly Lady Caroline Lamb. She preferred Lord Byron, and being Lady Caroline, she let the whole world know it. She dressed as a postboy and rode pillion on Byron's carriage, broke into his house, and slashed her wrists in the middle of a dinner party to get his attention. Melbourne tried to reason with her—that fatal masculine error—but it did no good. He learned his lesson from his stormy marriage, however, and never made the same mistake again. He used the carrot and the stick on Queen Victoria and it worked beautifully. He did not hide his male chauvinism from her, saying things like, "No woman should put pen to paper because they have too much passion and too little sense." This could not have set well with a compulsive diarist like Victoria, but he atoned for it with lavish hand-patting praise. "You did it beautifully!" he told her after her Coronation, when she was worried about her show of nervousness. If a woman were to fall headfirst down a flight of stairs, a woman's man could convince her that she had made the greatest entrance of her career. His mastery of "Now, now" (pat-pat) can make any contretemps go away.

Victoria had a Mr. Finklestein, too. Disraeli could wrap her around his little finger and spoon-feed her anything he wanted, but Gladstone could not. He rubbed her the wrong way, and she punctuated him to death in her diaries: "I never could take Mr. Gladstone as my minister again, for I never COULD have the slightest *particle* of confidence in Mr. Gladstone *after* his violent, mischievous and dangerous conduct for the last three years."

Lizzie Borden was not known for her ability to get along with men. We can safely assume that she did not have a good relationship with her father. On the day of the double hatchet murder, she managed to insult and alienate most of the Fall River, Massachusetts, police force after having already insulted and alienated the druggist from whom she had tried to buy poison a few days before. At her inquest, she snapped at the district attorney until he blew his stack, and so offended her uncle that he gave an interview in which he named her as the murderer. Hardly the girlish type—her profile has been described as "menacing"—we would expect her to be immune to masculine wiles, but she was not. Her defense attorney, former Massachusetts governor George Robinson, set her all aquiver in two minutes. Taking her hand, he patted it—naturally—and said, "It's going to be all right, little girl." Lizzie was thirty-two, but to a woman's man, every female is a little girl. During her trial, Lizzie was often seen talking to Robinson from behind her fan in an arch manner that no one had ever seen her use before. Robinson got her off, but the moment she was set free she reverted to character in her dealings with men. She packed up all the trial exhibits, including the photographs of her hacked-up parents, and sent them to the district attorney with a note saying, "as a memento of an interesting occasion."

Jonathan Stuart Mill would love to be a woman's man but he goes about it all wrong. His shoulder-to-shoulder egalitarian approach destroys sexual chemistry; he is simply not *manly* enough—a quality somewhat different from mere masculinity. As Joseph Lash comments in *Eleanor and Franklin*, Mrs. Roosevelt was charmed by Sergeant Earl Miller because "his helpfulness and brusque gallantries, and his barracks-room language, his cynicism, and his roughneck qualities were a new and interesting experience. . . . And to be squired around by this

handsome state trooper who paid her small masculine atten-
tions and treated her as a woman appealed to long dormant
feminine qualities in her. She even liked his lapses into a
roughness . . . considered rudeness."

Jonathan needs to get it through his head that a slap on the
behind once in a while is a viable alternative. That ultraliberal
woman's man, FDR, was well aware of the value of this *lèse
majesté*. Commented daughter Anna: "If Father became friendly
with a princess or a secretary, he'd reach out and give a pat to
her fanny and laugh like hell and was probably telling a funny
story at the same time. . . ."

Another American statesman who seems to have been a
woman's man is Henry Adams. Like Melbourne, his marriage
was tragic; Mrs. Adams committed suicide. Yet in his essay
"The Dynamo and the Virgin," he bridges the Madonna-
Whore gap that prevents so many men from understanding
women. Adams, a Protestant, mourned the absence of goddesses in American life: "An American Virgin would never
dare command; an American Venus would never dare exist."
He felt that we needed both the Virgin and Venus because "the
power of the goddess motivates men to their best." Such
understanding and acceptance of the duality of the feminine
nature is an identifying mark of the woman's man.

The woman's man can not only get away with male chauvinism, but he can make a woman like it. Some men are so smug
and condescending that they can make even "Hello" sound
chauvinistic. Others, like Jonathan Stuart Mill, talk so much
about sexual equality that it becomes meaningless and suspect.
The woman's man does not trouble to conceal his take-charge
manner. It is one of life's great comforts to hear him say, "Now,
sit down and *listen*." Such ultimatums are always followed up
with a "Now, now" (pat-pat). This is the man to be in a *Titanic*
lifeboat with. Jonathan Stuart Mill would need help with the
rowing.

Women remain susceptible to the woman's man even into their dotage. Two of the greatest woman's men of our era have been Arthur Godfrey and Bishop Fulton J. Sheen. The power that Godfrey wielded over old ladies was almost disgraceful. He was the only man I ever knew who could dominate Granny. She thought every word he uttered was a pearl beyond price and sat in front of the television making cooing noises like a turtledove. Today, Phil Donahue seems to be the new Godfrey. Personally, I can't "see" him, but I succumbed to Bishop Sheen along with the old ladies when I was fifteen. It was his satanic eyes.

14

THE ONE AND ONLY
MONTY WOOLLEY
or The Confirmed Bachelor

Monty's mother tried to keep the umbilical cord taut but it didn't work. He was too strong for her. When she dressed him in a sweet little suit and sent him off to school, the other boys tried to beat him up but that didn't work, either. Monty beat them up. Mrs. Woolley's next move was calculated invalidism, but whenever she wailed, "Son, I'm ill!" Monty said, "Go to the doctor." Finally she did. When she came home, she got into bed and motioned Monty to her side. In a weak voice she asked, "What would you do if I died?" Monty replied, "Call the undertaker. It's against the law to keep a body over three days."

She did not turn him into a Little Lord Fauntleroy or a homosexual, but she did manage one victory: she made him hate women so much that he never married. There is a slight catch that she didn't count on, however: he hates *her* too.

Naturally she lives to be ninety, but she doesn't live with Monty. He won't have it. He would like to put her in a barrel and drop her over Niagara Falls but he can't, so he puts her in her own apartment and keeps the family house for himself. Here, in solitary glory, he lives a pleasant, even elegant, guilt-free life. He visits "the old gorgon" once a week, chiefly to see if she's dead yet. He does what appears to be thoughtful, son-like things for her, like buying her the best hearing aid on the market. The other old ladies admire it and secretly envy her for having such a wonderful son, but they don't know Monty. He bought it to make things easier on himself and save his vocal chords.

Mrs. Woolley knows this, so she deliberately forgets to put her hearing aid in, or else she puts it in and deliberately forgets to turn it on, so Monty ends up yelling anyway. He gets so used to yelling at his mother that he develops the habit of yelling at all women.

Because his mother is simply a pest rather than a castrating threat, Monty's misogyny is refreshing and delightful rather than insulting and cruel. He never makes brutal jokes about menstruation or whines that women are as "false as Cressid." Instead he snaps, "Women are always washing things!" He is convinced that living with a woman prevents a man from shaving properly because the bathroom mirror is always steamed up. The click of knitting needles gets on his nerves, and any form of needlework drives him wild. "The air is full of lint! I can't breathe!" The female voice, even a resonate con-tralto, affects him like a new piece of chalk on a blackboard. One of his favorite theories is that the female voice always scales up when a woman talks for a long period of time; therefore no woman should be a lawyer or a broadcaster.

Monty belongs to the No Woman Can club. "No woman can cook a fish properly." Unlike the insecure man who associates steak with masculinity, Monty opts instead for fish, probably because life on a whaling ship—three years away from all women—is his idea of gracious living. He is a fisherman him-self, though he does not usually go out with his buddies—he may not have any, because he is often a misanthrope as well as a misogynist. A sportsman rather than an outdoorsman because he is fastidious, he likes to go alone and have everything the way he wants it. He prefers to bring his catch back home and cook it in his neat, well-organized, but very spartan kitchen. He is a superb cook. A little butter, a little salt, and that's that. No lemon juice, no tartar sauce, nothing French; just perfectly cooked fish.

"No woman can filet a fish." Monty's dexterity is awesome, yet he doesn't own a fish knife. He does it with two forks, and when he gets through there isn't a bone to be found. "No woman can open an oyster." Monty does not own an oyster knife; he uses a screwdriver. He can crack a crab and dismantle a lobster without making the usual mess, and he always refuses the restaurant's bib when he has lobster with lemon butter. He attributes his dexterity to the calm nerves that go with bachelorhood.

I knew a Monty who had three sisters. I was a friend of one of them, so the four of us went to Monty's house for dinner. It was during the trial of Lieutenant Calley. We women began to discuss the trial and give opinions. Monty sat in silence, making those standard gestures that Montys make when they find themselves in "a gaggle of hens." He crossed and recrossed his legs, pulled at his lip, folded his arms, and stared at the ceiling. Finally he slapped his palm on the table and said, "None of you know what you're talking about. You've never been to war, so keep quiet." We changed the subject.

Monty's are early-to-bed types, a habit they have acquired from long years of avoiding mixed-company gatherings like dances. When Monty decides that he wants to go to bed, all the etiquette books on earth will not stop him. He rose, nodded brusquely at his sisters and me, and said, "Don't forget to turn out the lights when you leave."

Monty's favorite books are *Beau Geste, The Count of Monte Cristo, Papillon,* and *Dry Guillotine.* Anything about men in prison appeals to him, the remoter the prison the better. His record collection leans toward all-male Welsh choirs singing

"Men of Harlech." He also has a well-worn disc entitled *Brass, Brass, Brass*. He is the type who reads all the descriptive notes on the back of the album before playing the record. Reality is Monty's beat; getting lost in music is for aesthetes. He wants to know what he is *going* to hear before he hears it. He buys the complete *Il Trovatore* and plays nothing but "The Anvil Chorus." That section of the record is gray; the rest is shiny black. He looked through the libretto, came to the stage direction *Leonora falls senseless*, and said "Hrrumph!"

He is thorough to the point of compulsiveness. If he buys a record with a flügelhorn on it, he will look up *flügelhorn* in the encyclopedia to find out who invented it, who composed for it, and who the great flügelhorn players have been.

He is a born ferreter. If he hears "The Kashmiri Song," also known as "Pale Hands I Loved Beside the Shalimar," the fact that the lover compares his sweetheart's hands to lotus petals disgusts him, but he gets very interested in the song itself. He wants to know *why* it has two titles, and *what* it all means. He knows that Shalimar is a perfume because once, when he went downtown to buy himself his yearly supply of twelve pairs of white boxer shorts, he got turned around in the store and found himself in the perfume department.

He looks *Kashmiri* and *Shalimar* up in his encyclopedia but does not find the answer, so the next day he goes to the library. Merely setting foot in the library puts him in a grumpy mood because so many women work there. After much snapping of pages and slamming of card file drawers, he finds the reference. He goes to the shelf to find the book but it's not there. Instead he finds a little sign saying that books in this section must be obtained from the librarian, so he stamps over to her desk and says, "I'M LOOKING FOR THE PLEASURE GARDENS OF INDIA!" The librarian jumps out of her skin, because women are unstable creatures.

It turns out that the book Monty wants is a bit naughty, so it cannot be checked out. Grumping and muttering, he takes it into the reading room and grimly plows through yeasty page after yeasty page until he finds the *facts* that he came for.

Monty's sex life? He could not be the way he is if he were highly sexed. His drive tends to atrophy by early middle age. In his youth he patronized prostitutes every payday. He looked upon these visits as necessary errands, like picking up his shirts at the laundry. Being Monty, he always stopped by the laundry first, so he invariably arrived at the brothel with a brown-wrapped package under his arm. If he was in the service during World War II, he stood in line with all the other GI's at the pleasure gardens of Hawaii. The line never moved fast enough to suit him because "Women are always late!"

The fun really starts when he enters the hospital to have his appendix out. His mother insists that he get a private phone. When Mrs. Woolley calls and the nurse answers and tells him it's his mother, he replies: "Tell her I'm dead." Nurse-ese drives him up the wall: "What do you mean it's time for *us* to eat? I wouldn't have dinner with you if you were the last woman on earth!" He refuses to take his medicine, spits out thermometers, and calls all the nurses cows.

They ought to hate him, but they don't. They love him, and come back for more insults. He invariably becomes the sweetheart of Surgery. Something girlish comes over the nurses, who giggle constantly and tell each other, "Isn't he adorable?"

It is one of the great ironies of human nature that men like Monty should appeal so to women, but they do. Especially now, when so many men seem to be falling apart. Monty makes a woman feel warm and secure and extremely womanly; he makes her think of starched white shirts, vests, suspenders, sock garters, paired military brushes, shaving mugs, leather furniture, hunting prints, and roll-top desks.

Unfortunately, there are fewer and fewer Montys as time goes by. It has taken courage to be a bona fide Monty since

1950, when Kinsey published *Sexual Behavior in the Human Male.* Until then, most people did not know much if anything about homosexuality. It was thought to be an esoteric aberration of ballet dancers, hairdressers, designers, and foreigners. When Kinsey announced that nearly half of all men had had some sort of homosexual encounter at least once in their lives, Americans stopped enjoying the confirmed bachelor and began to wonder about him.

Then came the Organization Man of the Fifties, who not only had to be married, he had to bring his wife along to his final interview before he got the job. Corporations put incredible pressure on bachelors to marry, and if they did not, they might be hounded out of the "team."

America's either-or sexual steamroller is still at work. Today a man is either straight or gay, and if he belongs to the former category, he must be either a playboy or a husband. Monty is as straight as an arrow, but few people today would believe it, or leave him in peace.

Our present touchy-feely national mood is also inimical to the care and preservation of Montys in our midst. Everyone must be friendly. Gruffness, Monty's most endearing quality, is out. Monty also tends to be formal in an Old World sort of way, and that is most definitely out. Monty would pay no attention to the cheery reminder on his credit card statement that his Personal Service Representative is "Fran." If he wrote a letter to her, he would begin with a frosty "Dear Madam."

Nowadays, the confirmed bachelor is turning into the divorced bachelor, like Felix Unger. They have some characteristics in common, but generally speaking, Felix is a poor substitute for the real article.

It is not always necessary to be a bachelor to be a Monty. Any man whose teeth are set on edge by "intense" women is a possible candidate. Nathaniel Hawthorne was such a man. His intense woman was Margaret Fuller, whom he absolutely despised. The mere mention of her name made his eyes roll. He hated her so much that he wrote *The Blithedale Romance*, his novel about a Transcendentalist commune, partly for the pleasure of satirizing her. She is the "dark and passionate" Zenobia, "dark and passionate" being a Monty code for zealous reforming females. Any woman with a bee in her bonnet, like Eleanor Roosevelt or Bella Abzug, brings out the Monty in men.

Could Monty bear any woman at all? Looking through history, I think he would like Madame de Maintenon, the morganatic wife of Louis XIV. She was extremely intelligent and "sensible"—a favorite Monty word—and most of all she was pharisaical. Monty likes rigid women who disapprove of nearly everything because they are the only women who say "Hrrumph!"

15

MEN IN DISTRESS
or The Age of Male Vulnerability

Men talk a lot about female vulnerability but they worry more
about their own. The subject obsessed the mysterious Dr.
Tower in Henry Bellamann's novel *Kings Row*. Probing the
beginnings of emotional disturbance and insanity, Tower concluded that the thirteenth century was the last sane century in
the history of the world. After that came modern discoveries in
astronomy and science that put an end to man as the center of
things. Tower reflected:

> The vanity of man couldn't stand it.... What was really
> threatened was the happiness and peace of mind of all man-
> kind. Man was happy in his place of importance and when it
> was shaken he was too weak and scared ever really to have a
> sound sleep again. He simply couldn't stand it. Man breaks
> down under the strain of bewilderment and disappointment
> and disillusionment. He goes crazy, commits suicide, and all
> such things. Since the thirteenth century, man's chief prob-
> lem has been lacerated vanity.

There is something to this theory. The thirteenth century
exerts a curious hold over men. A minor American classic is

James J. Walsh's *The Thirteenth: Greatest of All Centuries*, and the
early medieval period intrigued Henry Adams all of his life.
Women are too pragmatic to care whether the sun revolves
around the earth or vice versa, and the medieval woman was
too busy keeping frolicksome Crusaders and lecherous priests
from revolving too closely around *her* to worry about intangi-
bles like real satellites. But to men, this question of a larger
centrality is directly related to their self-image.

The demise of the ballsy thirteenth was nothing compared to
the advent of our era of sexual revolution. A television commercial for feminine hygiene products claims that the seventies are a
great time to be a woman. They are a bad time to be a man.

In the last ten years or so, men have been beset by some of
the bluntest women in history—Galileos with tits, so to speak.
Before the advent of Jacqueline Susann, a woman who came
across the word *kip* in a novel would have consulted an atlas for
a Persian satrapy or a river in the Punjab. Miss. Susann straightened that one out. Her sledgehammer style pounded away at
men in observations like: "He's in his late fifties and he drinks.
That combination is murder. You'll have to start right off giving
him head."

Then along came Germaine Greer. There were feminist
books before *The Female Eunuch* but they were not written by
matey Australians. Miss Greer has a habit of making a lofty,
august statement like: "Man demands in his arrogance to be
loved as he is," and following it with a bugger-you-Jack clar-
ification: "pot-belly, wattles, bad breath, farting, stubble, bald-
ness and other ugliness."

Female tact has become an endangered virtue. America contains untold copies of *The New Impotence* with yogurt-stained
pages—it's a favorite lunchtime book that women read in full
view of the men in their offices. They also read those lugubrious case histories of Mark, Ted, Jerry, and Bill, who confess
their worries about penile size, premature ejaculation, and
rejection. There is no end to such books thanks to that hand-

maiden of the media known as the "spin-off." We have come a long way from the mere sequel. In days gone by we indulged in *Thunderhead, Son of Flicka* and then dropped the subject. Now we have Mark, Ted, Jerry, and Bill in *Impotence, Impotence II, More Impotence,* and *The Compleat Impotence.* Today's woman is tripping the Hite fantastic and men know it. Her Poor Peter Pecker books are strewn all over the office.

The theme of men dominating men that is currently enjoying a vogue in novels and movies has thrown men for a loop. The theme is not new; the schoolyard bully and the sadistic sergeant have been stock characters for a long time, but the seventies script has been changed. We are now living in the *Deliverance* decade; the bully has gone from mugger to bugger.

James Dickey's male-on-male rape scene was a turning point for the American man. He has not been the same since. Ben Haas' new novel, *The House of Christina,* goes even further, though in a symbolic way, in its description of Cossack atrocities committed against Austrian troops in World War I:

> Three of the men were still alive, past screaming now, but pleading in hoarse whispers for an end to their irremediable agony. . . . There were rules for the treatment of prisoners of war, but the Cossacks made their own rules. They had driven fourteen strong wooden stakes into the cold red earth, with sharp ends pointed upwards. Had dragged the uniform trousers and underclothes off each man, had bound hands behind their backs, ankles together, and then they had impaled each Austrian through the anus by forcing him down on a stake, ramming the wood brutally up through the bowels. After which, the Cossacks retreated, leaving their victims to die with agonizing slowness as their own weight forced the points upward through the vitals.

A movie that most of America saw, taken from a novel that most of America later read, is *Rich Man, Poor Man.* The story is dominated by the overpowering presence of the most menacing intersexual archvillain of all time, Falconetti. When Falconetti rapes a merchant seaman, the seaman's best friend, Tom Jordache, takes revenge in a fight in which he gouges out one of Falconetti's eyes. The friendship which inspired Tom to fight is moving, but the episode was bound to leave the male viewer with a disturbing thought: not only do men rape men, but other men play Saint George and avenge the victim's honor. It is too close to the traditional male-female drama for comfort.

These frank fictional treatments of male-on-male dominance have been accompanied by similar real-life incidents. We have seen the "Trashcan murders" in Los Angeles, the mass murder of men and boys in Houston, and the epidemic rise in male prostitution that has necessitated the inclusion of males in the previously "all-female" Mann Act.

The seventies man has been forced to see himself in a feminine role, as a potential victim of male sexual violence. Many feminists are frankly delighted that men are now learning how the other half lives. They relish the spectacle of men guarding their orifices; to the most radical feminists, it is not only the sine qua non of sexual equality but the very quintessence of the American Dream: "Everybody has a right to a fate worse than death."

Men have been further threatened in recent years by the demise of symbolic masculinity. The warrior has always been the supreme symbol of masculinity. Today, for the first time in American history, the warrior is persona non grata. The Vietnam veteran has been incredibly abused. Most people assume that he is insane, or a drug addict, and the media have helped strengthen such attitudes. There is a TV movie called *Stanley* about a Viet vet who becomes so alienated that he collects and trains pet rattlesnakes to kill his enemies. When Johnny comes slithering home to fare like this, all men suffer a drop in their self-image.

That other symbol of masculinity, the doctor, has taken an equally bad beating. Like men in general, doctors were once looked up to in fear and trembling, but now they are being sued right and left—a castration of sorts that many feminists have cheered on sexual rather than purely medical grounds.

The subject of homosexuality is as pervasive and ubiquitous as Los Angeles smog. The seventies have seen both the Gay and the Antigay movements. No other subject has had such nonstop attention in America since the Prohibition movement, when we divided ourselves into the Wets and the Drys. Now we are once again dividing ourselves into the Wets and the Drys on the gay question. Whichever side you are on, or if you are on no side, the subject is one that you cannot avoid or ignore.

Anita Bryant obviously stands foursquare behind heterosexual men, but her actions have only increased their vulnerability because her campaign rained on one of men's most important parades.

In an essay, "Come Back To the Raft Ag'in, Huck Honey!" Leslie Fiedler says:

The existence of overt homosexuality threatens to compromise an essential aspect of American sentimental life: the cameraderie of the locker room and ball park, the good fellowship of the poker game and fishing trip, a kind of passionless passion, at once gross and delicate, homoerotic in the boy's sense, possessing an innocence above suspicion. To doubt for a moment this innocence, which can survive only as *assumed*, would destroy our stubborn belief in a relationship simple, utterly satisfying, yet immune to lust; physical as the handshake is physical, this side of copulation. . . . From what other source could arise that air of good clean fun which overhangs such sessions? It is this self-congratulatory buddy-buddyness, its astonishing naiveté that breed at once endless opportunities for inversion and the terrible reluctance to admit its existence, to surrender the last believed-in stronghold of love without passion.

Miss Bryant deep-sixed the raft. Being against something attracts far more attention than being for something. Miss Bryant raised the specter of homosexuality in such a way that men who had previously been able to ignore it can now no longer do so. In addition, she put straight men to shame by taking what should have been their manly duty on her own shoulders. The average straight man feels in his heart that a *man* should have led the antigay movement. It is another Saint George situation; this time, Saint George is feminine and the dragon is effeminate. Miss Bryant relegated straight men to the castle window to wave their hankies while the battle rages below. One would have expected her to become the sweetheart of the straight male community, for she certainly is attractive. She is also pious, which normally brings out the rogue in a man: seducing a pillar of the church is a favorite male fantasy. Yet aside from her male disciples, straight men have been decidedly cool toward her. Her greatest popularity has been among other women: *Good Housekeeping* readers voted her their most admired woman.

That uniquely seventyish institution, the singles bar, also poses a homosexual threat to men. Ironically, singles bars are disturbingly like gay bars. Both are gin mills with a primarily sexual function. Their atmospheres are identical: anonymity, false happiness, frantic conviviality or a studied blasé pose adopted to mask desperation, a concentration on physical attractiveness and youth, mockery or harsh pity toward anyone "over the hill," and an underlying sense of stealth and guilt.

The woman a man meets in a singles bar seems eerily "male" to him. Generally she is on the prowl: she is seeking sex for physical satisfaction, she is barren because she is on the Pill, she sits alone at bars, she knocks back booze like an established toper, and she will settle for a one-night stand. Sterile sex, transitory sex, anonymous sex, emotionally detached sex, and blatantly physical sex all suggest homosexuality on a subconscious level. Thus when a man picks up such a woman and sleeps with her, the experience is, psychologically speaking, a quasi-homosexual one. He comes away from such encounters with damaged self-esteem and increased doubts about the virility that he may not have been very sure of in the first place.

Lest this theory seem farfetched, observe the appallingly crude behavior and language that men so often exhibit in singles bars. It goes beyond liberation. It is a good indication that on an unconscious level, they feel themselves to be in an all-male atmosphere.

The onslaughts of the seventies have driven many men into a situation that is the irony of ironies. Now that there are fewer women willing to devote their lives to what used to be called "the care and feeding of the male ego," men themselves have taken over this task, much the way some of them have taken over the care and feeding of their offspring while Mother goes to the office.

Some men have even fallen in love with their egos. The psychological process by which something abstract or nonexistent is viewed as material is called *reification*. Ernest G. Schachtel analyzes the reified ego in his essay "Alienated Concepts of Identity." With such men, "the ego tends to dominate the whole life. They are haunted by their ego and no longer seem to feel that they have a life apart from their ego, but they stand or fall with it." Such a man "is always threatened with the danger of losing this 'thing' on which his self-esteem is based and is subject to the feeling that without the prop of such an attribute, he could not live."

What we now call macho is really the reified ego. The man who looks at his ego in this way commits a form of suicide. It is not *he* who is he; his *ego* is he. It is a case of the self destroyed by

the ego, a nightmarish conundrum that makes mere schizo-
phrenia seem like a mild facial tic. Instead of the Latin "I am,"
the macho man has an "it is."

The televised political scandals of the seventies have just
about destroyed the male's old feelings of manly dignity. We
are living in the age of men in distress, and there are no
d'Artagnans under kleig lights. Men were roasted in the Rump
Parliament and the Spartan Council of Ephors, too, but there
were no media then, so women did not see sweat-dappled male
brows or hear fear-tightened male voices. Today's American
woman has a steady diet of wilted men for her edification, and
men know it. No wonder she devours historical novels. Could
you have sweet savage passion with Bert Lance?

I do not particularly care about getting more women into
office. I would settle for more men. America's love affair with
the lowest common denominator has killed the princely image.
With the exception of John F. Kennedy, whose Camelot image
has now been tarnished, our elected officials have been floundering buffoons and melancholic small-town Rasputins. There
are no men to stir the blood or make the heart beat faster. In the
past, we managed to produce some larger-than-life floundering
buffoons like William Jennings Bryan, but now we cannot even
seem to manage that. We have now reached the nadir in Jimmy
Carter, with his Father's Day sweaters, his onerous plebianism,
his tasteless informality, and his curious urges to spend the
night with total strangers. I hope he doesn't take a notion to
spend the night with me—that's *all* I need.

As for Brother Billy, watching him on television is like anal
intercourse: once is enough, after that, your curiosity is satisfied.

16

THE MASTERPIECE
THEATRE MAN
or "Let Me Call
You Sweetheart"

If any woman ought to be a feminist, it is I. I have been on my own since I graduated from college, and I have suffered most of the slings and arrows in the male quiver. I have never been supported by a man. Somehow or other, I always managed to support myself and to live alone. As I write this, it is 5:30 A.M. and no man is saying, "What the hell do you think you're doing?" so I suppose I am liberated.

I am in favor of most feminist goals and I realize how much the Woman's Movement has accomplished, but I cannot take any more cacophony, buttons, tee shirts, Hite reports, anti-Hite reports, unbrassiered bosoms, task forces, and fractured English. I long for the good old days when *alternative* had no plural.

When a woman watching a feminist panel discussion finds herself asking, "Oh, God, what do women want?" it is a sign that something is terribly wrong. The feminists have made a fatal error that the Suffragettes were wise enough to avoid: they have scattered their shot. The Suffragettes went after one thing, the vote. They reasoned that if they got it, they could then use it to obtain their other goals. The feminists have entered so many frays with flaming swords that I can only conclude that the All-Purpose Feminist Goal is an abortion performed by a gay black doctor under an endangered tree on an Indian reservation.

No matter how bad the feminists get, the antifeminists are always one step ahead of them. I cannot take any more *Stop ERA* aprons, bake-offs in the state legislature, crucified dolls, bloody fetus photo albums, or Marabel Morgan, who believes that wives should leap out of bed after intercourse and clap their hands to applaud their husbands' performance. *Post coitum omnis animal asinus est.* The antifeminists are guilty of even more lapses in taste than the feminists. The worst lapse is the marriage between antifeminism and muscular Christianity. I do not believe that Jesus was the son of God. As Granny used to say: "Girls in occupied countries are always getting in trouble with soldiers. It happened to my Aunt Sarah after the War of Northern Aggression." Nonetheless, He is *supposed* to be divine, which makes gossipy Fundamentalist revelations like, "I was talking to Jesus the other day and He told me that the man should be the head of the house" frankly blasphemous.

America needs a new decade, and we need it fast. In the fifties the watchword was "If you love him, you won't." In the sixties it was "If you love him, you will." In the seventies it is "Frighten the horses."

I hope the eighties will prove to be the Masterpiece Theatre decade, with a return to glamour and elegance in relations between the sexes. I thought I had passed the age for crushes but I have gone positively gaga over Alistair Cooke. In this heyday of fantasies, he is the star of mine. We are having *tea* in the Palm Court of the Plaza Hotel while a chamber orchestra plays Victor Herbert medleys and the theme from "Upstairs, Downstairs." He is wearing a wing collar and I am wearing a huge, smashing hat circa 1910.

The Masterpiece Theatre man has become a saviour for women who have no wish to frighten the horses. Would Mr. Hudson say, "I'd like to get it on with you?" Would Emperor Claudius say, "Our r-r-relationship isn't v-v-v-viable?" I think not.